Table Of Contents

The Secret Makers: Unveiling the Truth behind the Federal Reserve

1.1 The Need for a Central Bank

A central bank is an institution that plays a crucial role in the functioning of a country's economy. It is responsible for managing the nation's money supply, controlling interest rates, and ensuring the stability of the financial system. The establishment of a central bank is often seen as a necessary step in the development of a modern economy. In the case of the United States, the need for a central bank became apparent in the late 19th and early 20th centuries.

During this period, the United States experienced significant economic growth and expansion. Industrialization was transforming the nation, and the economy was becoming increasingly complex. However, the lack of a central authority to regulate and stabilize the financial system posed numerous challenges. Without a central bank, the country's monetary policy was fragmented, and there was no unified mechanism to address economic crises or control the money supply.

One of the primary reasons for the establishment of a central bank was the need for a stable currency. Prior to the creation of the Federal Reserve, the United States had a decentralized banking system, with thousands of independent banks issuing their own currency. This system led to frequent bank failures, currency fluctuations, and a lack of confidence in the financial system. The absence of a central authority to oversee and regulate the banking sector made it difficult to maintain a stable and reliable currency.

Another important factor that contributed to the need for a central bank was the desire to address the issue of financial panics. Throughout the 19th century, the United States experienced several severe economic crises, known as panics, which caused widespread bank failures, unemployment, and economic downturns. These panics were often triggered by speculative bubbles, excessive lending, and a lack of coordination among banks. The absence of a central bank meant that there was no institution with the authority and resources to act as a lender of last resort and provide liquidity during times of crisis.

Furthermore, the lack of a central bank meant that the United States had limited control over its monetary policy. The country's money supply was largely influenced by international factors, such as the supply of gold and silver, as well as the actions of foreign central banks. This lack of control over monetary policy made it difficult for the United States to pursue its economic objectives and respond effectively to domestic economic conditions.

The creation of the Federal Reserve in 1913 was a response to these challenges. The Federal Reserve Act established a central bank with the authority to regulate and supervise the banking system, control the money supply, and act as a lender of last resort. The Federal Reserve was designed to provide stability to the financial system, ensure the availability of credit, and promote economic growth.

However, the establishment of the Federal Reserve also brought about a shift in power dynamics. Prior to its creation, the American people had a certain degree of power over the government through mechanisms such as veto power. The decentralized banking system allowed for a more localized control over the economy, with individual banks having a significant influence over their respective regions. This gave the American people a certain level of control and influence over the financial system.

With the creation of the Federal Reserve, power shifted to a centralized authority. The Federal Reserve became the sole institution responsible for monetary policy and had the authority to regulate and supervise the banking system. This centralization of power reduced the influence of individual banks and the American people over the financial system. The Federal Reserve's decisions on interest rates, money supply, and financial regulations became the primary drivers of the economy, with limited input from the public.

While the establishment of the Federal Reserve was met with some opposition, it is important to note that not all presidents sought to end it. President John F. Kennedy is often cited as one of the presidents who attempted to challenge the Federal Reserve. However, it is important to clarify that Kennedy's opposition to the Federal Reserve was not aimed at ending it but rather at reforming its structure and policies. Kennedy was concerned about the concentration of power within the Federal Reserve and sought to increase transparency and accountability.

Other presidents, such as Andrew Jackson and Woodrow Wilson, also expressed concerns about the power of central banks but did not actively seek to end the Federal Reserve. Instead, they focused on implementing reforms and regulations to address their concerns. The outcome of presidential opposition to the Federal Reserve has varied throughout history. While some presidents were successful in implementing certain reforms, the overall structure and existence of the Federal Reserve remained intact.

In conclusion, the need for a central bank in the United States became apparent due to the challenges posed by a decentralized banking system, frequent financial panics, and a lack of control over monetary policy. The establishment of the Federal Reserve aimed to address these issues and provide stability to the financial system. However, this centralization of power also resulted in a shift in power dynamics, reducing the influence of the American people over the financial system. While some presidents, including JFK, expressed opposition to the Federal Reserve, their efforts focused on reform rather than ending its existence. The outcome of presidential opposition has varied, with some successful reforms implemented but the overall structure of the Federal Reserve remaining intact.

1.2 The Creation of the Federal Reserve

The creation of the Federal Reserve, the central banking system of the United States, was a significant event in American history. To understand its origins, it is essential to delve into the circumstances that led to its establishment and the motivations behind it.

The Need for a Central Bank

In the late 19th and early 20th centuries, the United States experienced a series of financial crises and economic instability. The absence of a centralized banking system meant that each state and individual bank operated independently, leading to a lack of coordination and regulation. This decentralized system resulted in frequent bank failures, currency shortages, and economic downturns.

Recognizing the need for a more stable and efficient financial system, various individuals and organizations advocated for the establishment of a central bank. The primary objectives were to provide a stable currency, regulate the banking industry, and act as a lender of last resort during times of financial stress.

The Creation of the Federal Reserve Act

The Federal Reserve Act, which established the Federal Reserve System, was signed into law by President Woodrow Wilson on December 23, 1913. The act was the culmination of years of debate and political maneuvering.

The Federal Reserve Act created a decentralized central banking system consisting of twelve regional banks, overseen by a Board of Governors in Washington, D.C. The regional banks were intended to represent the interests of different parts of the country and ensure that monetary policy decisions were not solely controlled by Wall Street or the federal government.

The Men Behind the Federal Reserve

The creation of the Federal Reserve involved the collaboration of various influential figures from the worlds of finance, politics, and academia. The key individuals involved in its establishment were Senator Nelson Aldrich, Paul Warburg, Benjamin Strong, and President Woodrow Wilson.

Senator Nelson Aldrich, a Republican senator from Rhode Island and the chairman of the National Monetary Commission, played a crucial role in shaping the legislation that led to the creation of the Federal Reserve. He worked closely with bankers and economists to develop a plan that would address the country's financial challenges.

Paul Warburg, a German-born banker and partner at Kuhn, Loeb & Co., was a prominent advocate for the establishment of a central bank in the United States. He brought his expertise in central banking systems from Europe and played a significant role in shaping the structure and functions of the Federal Reserve.

Benjamin Strong, a banker and the first Governor of the Federal Reserve Bank of New York, was instrumental in implementing the policies and practices of the Federal Reserve. His leadership and influence helped establish the Federal Reserve as a powerful institution within the American financial system.

President Woodrow Wilson, who signed the Federal Reserve Act into law, supported the establishment of a central bank to address the country's financial instability. Wilson believed that a central bank would provide stability, regulate the banking industry, and promote economic growth.

The Goals and Objectives of the Federal Reserve

The primary goals of the Federal Reserve, as outlined in the Federal Reserve Act, were to promote maximum employment, stable prices, and moderate long-term interest rates. The Federal Reserve was tasked with conducting monetary policy, supervising and regulating banks, and providing financial services to the government and financial institutions.

One of the key objectives of the Federal Reserve was to act as a lender of last resort during times of financial stress. By providing liquidity to banks and the financial system, the Federal Reserve aimed to prevent bank runs and stabilize the economy during periods of economic downturn.

Additionally, the Federal Reserve was responsible for regulating and supervising banks to ensure the safety and soundness of the banking system. It had the authority to set reserve requirements, conduct bank examinations, and enforce banking regulations.

In conclusion, the creation of the Federal Reserve was a response to the need for a centralized banking system in the United States. The collaboration of influential figures such as Senator Nelson Aldrich, Paul Warburg, Benjamin Strong, and President Woodrow Wilson led to the establishment of the Federal Reserve System. Its primary goals were to provide stability to the financial system, regulate banks, and promote economic growth. Understanding the origins and objectives of the Federal Reserve is crucial in comprehending its role and impact on the American economy and society.

1.3 The Men Behind the Federal Reserve

The creation of the Federal Reserve was not a decision made by a single individual, but rather the result of a collective effort by a group of influential men. Understanding the motivations and backgrounds of these individuals is crucial in unraveling the true history behind the Federal Reserve.

One of the key figures behind the establishment of the Federal Reserve was Paul Warburg, a German-born American banker. Warburg was a partner in the prominent banking firm Kuhn, Loeb & Co. and had a deep understanding of the European banking system. He played a pivotal role in shaping the structure and functions of the Federal Reserve, drawing inspiration from the central banks of Europe.

Another influential figure was Nelson Aldrich, a Republican senator from Rhode Island and the chairman of the National Monetary Commission. Aldrich was known for his close ties to the banking industry and his belief in the need for a centralized banking system in the United States. He led the commission's efforts to study and propose solutions to the country's banking problems, which ultimately laid the groundwork for the creation of the Federal Reserve.

Benjamin Strong, the first Governor of the Federal Reserve Bank of New York, also played a significant role in the establishment of the Federal Reserve. Strong was a trusted ally of J.P. Morgan, one of the most powerful bankers of his time. His close relationship with Morgan and his expertise in monetary policy made him a key player in the formation and early operations of the Federal Reserve.

Other notable individuals involved in the creation of the Federal Reserve include Henry P. Davison, a senior partner at J.P. Morgan & Co., and Charles Hamlin, the first Chairman of the Federal Reserve Board. These men, along with others, worked together to draft the Federal Reserve Act and navigate its passage through Congress.

Before the establishment of the Federal Reserve, the American people had certain powers over the government, including the power of veto. The president had the authority to veto legislation passed by Congress, which provided a check on the power of the legislative branch. However, the creation of the Federal Reserve shifted some of the power away from the American people and into the hands of the central bank.

With the establishment of the Federal Reserve, the power to control the nation's monetary policy was largely transferred from the government to the central bank. This meant that decisions regarding interest rates, money supply, and other key economic factors were now in the hands of unelected officials rather than elected representatives. As a result, the American people lost some of their direct influence over these important economic decisions.

In addition to President John F. Kennedy, who famously opposed the Federal Reserve and sought to dismantle it, several other presidents have expressed concerns about the central bank's power and influence. Presidents such as Andrew Jackson, Abraham Lincoln, and Woodrow Wilson all had reservations about the concentration of power in the hands of private bankers.

However, despite these oppositions, the Federal Reserve has remained intact and its power has continued to grow over the years. The central bank has proven to be resilient in the face of presidential opposition, largely due to its independence and the support it receives from the financial industry.

The outcome of presidential opposition to the Federal Reserve has varied. While some presidents, like Kennedy, were unable to achieve their goals of ending or significantly reforming the central bank, their opposition did bring attention to the issue and sparked public debate. In some cases, presidents have been able to appoint individuals to key positions within the Federal Reserve who share their views, which can influence the direction of the central bank's policies.

Overall, the men behind the Federal Reserve played a crucial role in its creation and shaping its functions. The American people had certain powers over the government before the establishment of the Federal Reserve, including veto power. However, the creation of the central bank shifted some of the power away from the people and into the hands of unelected officials. While several presidents have opposed the Federal Reserve, their opposition has had varying degrees of success in challenging the central bank's power and influence.

1.4 The Goals and Objectives of the Federal Reserve

The Federal Reserve, often referred to as the Fed, is the central banking system of the United States. Established in 1913, its creation was driven by a perceived need for a stable and flexible financial system that could effectively respond to economic crises. The goals and objectives of the Federal Reserve have evolved over time, reflecting the changing economic landscape and the challenges faced by the nation. In this section, we will explore the primary goals and objectives of the Federal Reserve and how they have shaped its role in the American economy.

The Dual Mandate

The Federal Reserve's primary goals are often referred to as the "dual mandate." These goals, as mandated by Congress, are to promote maximum employment and stable prices. The Federal Reserve aims to achieve maximum employment by fostering a healthy labor market and promoting sustainable economic growth. It seeks to maintain stable prices by keeping inflation in check and avoiding deflation, which can have detrimental effects on the economy.

Monetary Policy

One of the key tools the Federal Reserve uses to achieve its goals is monetary policy. Through its control over the money supply and interest rates, the Federal Reserve influences borrowing costs, spending, and investment decisions. By adjusting interest rates, the Fed can stimulate or slow down economic activity. Lowering interest rates encourages borrowing and spending, which can stimulate economic growth and job creation. Conversely, raising interest rates can help curb inflationary pressures and prevent the economy from overheating.

Financial Stability

In addition to its dual mandate, the Federal Reserve also has a responsibility to maintain the stability of the financial system. This objective gained prominence following the Great Depression in the 1930s and the more recent global financial crisis in 2008. The Federal Reserve acts as a lender of last resort, providing liquidity to banks and financial institutions during times of crisis to prevent widespread panic and systemic collapse. It also plays a crucial role in regulating and supervising banks to ensure their safety and soundness.

Economic Research and Data Analysis

Another important objective of the Federal Reserve is to conduct economic research and analysis. The Fed collects and analyzes vast amounts of data on various economic indicators, such as employment, inflation, and GDP growth. This research helps policymakers make informed decisions and provides valuable insights into the state of the economy. The Federal Reserve also publishes regular reports and economic forecasts, which serve as important tools for businesses, investors, and policymakers.

International Cooperation

While the Federal Reserve's primary focus is on the domestic economy, it also plays a significant role in the global financial system. The Fed collaborates with other central banks and international organizations to promote financial stability and cooperation. It participates in forums such as the G20 and the Bank for International Settlements to address global economic challenges and coordinate policy responses.

Balancing Independence and Accountability

The Federal Reserve operates with a degree of independence from the political process to insulate monetary policy decisions from short-term political pressures. This independence allows the Fed to make decisions based on economic data and analysis rather than political considerations. However, this independence also raises questions about accountability and transparency. Critics argue that the Federal Reserve should be subject to more oversight and scrutiny to ensure its actions align with the best interests of the American people.

In conclusion, the Federal Reserve has several goals and objectives that guide its actions and policies. Its dual mandate of promoting maximum employment and stable prices forms the foundation of its mission. Through monetary policy, financial stability efforts, economic research, and international cooperation, the Federal Reserve seeks to maintain a healthy and stable economy. However, the balance between independence and accountability remains a subject of debate, highlighting the need for ongoing discussions about the role and effectiveness of the Federal Reserve in the American economy.

The Power Dynamics Before and After the Federal Reserve

2.1 The American People's Power Before the Federal Reserve

Before the establishment of the Federal Reserve, the American people held a significant amount of power over the government, including the ability to influence policy decisions and exercise veto power. This section will explore the extent of their power and the subsequent loss of power after the creation of the Federal Reserve.

The Power of the American People

In the early years of the United States, the Founding Fathers designed a system of government that aimed to ensure the power remained in the hands of the people. The Constitution provided a framework for a representative democracy, where citizens could elect officials to make decisions on their behalf. This system allowed the American people to have a voice in the governance of the nation.

One of the key powers held by the American people was the ability to exercise veto power. Through the electoral process, citizens could elect representatives who aligned with their interests and values. These representatives had the authority to veto legislation that they believed did not serve the best interests of their constituents. This power allowed the American people to directly influence the laws and policies of the country.

Furthermore, the American people had the power to hold their elected officials accountable. Regular elections provided an opportunity for citizens to voice their approval or disapproval of the government's actions. If elected officials failed to meet the expectations of their constituents, they could be voted out of office, ensuring a level of accountability in the political system.

The Loss of Power After the Federal Reserve

The establishment of the Federal Reserve in 1913 marked a significant shift in the power dynamics between the American people and the government. With the creation of the central bank, a new entity was introduced that wielded considerable influence over the nation's monetary policy and financial system.

One of the key consequences of the Federal Reserve's establishment was the centralization of economic power. Prior to its creation, the American people had a more decentralized control over the nation's banking and financial system. Local banks played a crucial role in providing credit and financing to individuals and businesses, allowing for a more localized decision-making process. However, with the Federal Reserve's authority to regulate and control the banking system, this power was consolidated at the federal level.

Additionally, the Federal Reserve's ability to manipulate interest rates and regulate the money supply gave it significant influence over the economy. This centralized control over monetary policy meant that decisions regarding interest rates and the availability of credit were no longer solely in the hands of the American people. Instead, these decisions were made by a small group of appointed officials within the Federal Reserve, who were not directly accountable to the public.

Presidential Opposition to the Federal Reserve

John F. Kennedy (JFK) was not the only president to express opposition to the Federal Reserve. Throughout history, several presidents have questioned the role and influence of the central bank. For example, President Andrew Jackson was a vocal critic of central banking and vetoed the rechartering of the Second Bank of the United States in 1832. His opposition stemmed from concerns about the concentration of power and the potential for corruption within the banking system.

In more recent times, President Woodrow Wilson, who signed the Federal Reserve Act into law, expressed regret over his decision. He acknowledged that the Federal Reserve had become dominated by powerful banking interests and expressed concerns about the lack of democratic control over the central bank.

Despite these expressions of opposition, the Federal Reserve has remained intact, largely due to the entrenched interests and the complex web of financial and political relationships that surround it. The central bank has proven to be resilient in the face of presidential opposition, and attempts to dismantle or significantly alter its structure have been met with significant challenges.

Conclusion

Before the establishment of the Federal Reserve, the American people held a considerable amount of power over the government. They had the ability to exercise veto power through the electoral process and hold their elected officials accountable. However, with the creation of the Federal Reserve, power shifted towards a centralized authority, diminishing the influence of the American people over monetary policy and the financial system.

While some presidents, including JFK, expressed opposition to the Federal Reserve, their efforts to challenge or dismantle the central bank have been largely unsuccessful. The Federal Reserve remains a powerful institution, with significant control over the nation's economy. Understanding the historical context and the power dynamics surrounding the Federal Reserve is crucial in evaluating its impact on the American people and the need for potential reforms.

2.2 Veto Power and its Significance

Before the establishment of the Federal Reserve, the American people held a significant amount of power over the government, including the power of veto. The concept of veto power refers to the ability of the people to reject or block any proposed legislation or policy that they deemed unfavorable or against their interests. This power was derived from the democratic principles upon which the United States was founded.

In the early years of the nation, the American people had a direct say in the decision-making process through their elected representatives. The Constitution provided a system of checks and balances, ensuring that no single branch of government could become too powerful. This system allowed the people to exercise their veto power indirectly by electing officials who would represent their interests and act as a check on the government's actions.

However, with the establishment of the Federal Reserve in 1913, the power dynamics shifted significantly. The Federal Reserve Act granted the newly formed central bank a considerable amount of authority over the nation's monetary policy and financial system. This transfer of power from the people to a centralized institution had a profound impact on the American people's ability to exercise their veto power.

One of the key consequences of the Federal Reserve's establishment was the loss of direct control over the nation's money supply. Previously, the American people had the power to influence the government's fiscal decisions through their elected representatives. However, with the Federal Reserve's control over monetary policy, decisions regarding interest rates, inflation, and the overall health of the economy were now in the hands of a select group of unelected officials.

The loss of veto power was further exacerbated by the Federal Reserve's independence from political influence. Unlike other government agencies, the Federal Reserve operates with a significant degree of autonomy, shielding it from direct democratic control. This independence allows the Federal Reserve to make decisions based on its own assessment of economic conditions, often without direct input from the American people.

While the establishment of the Federal Reserve marked a significant shift in power dynamics, it is important to note that the American people still retain some influence over the government. The power to elect officials who can shape policy and advocate for change remains a fundamental aspect of democracy. However, the ability to directly veto specific policies or decisions related to monetary policy has been largely diminished.

Throughout history, there have been several presidents who expressed opposition to the Federal Reserve and its role in the economy. One notable example is President John F. Kennedy. Kennedy was critical of the Federal Reserve's influence and sought to curtail its power. He believed that the central bank's policies were contributing to inflation and economic instability. However, before he could enact any significant changes, Kennedy was assassinated in 1963, leaving his efforts unfinished.

Other presidents, such as Andrew Jackson and Woodrow Wilson, also expressed concerns about the concentration of power in the hands of the Federal Reserve. Jackson, in particular, was a staunch opponent of central banking and vetoed the rechartering of the Second Bank of the United States in 1832. His opposition to the central bank was rooted in his belief that it favored the wealthy elite at the expense of the common people.

Despite these oppositions, the Federal Reserve has remained intact and continues to play a significant role in shaping the nation's monetary policy. Over the years, the central bank has faced criticism from various quarters, but efforts to dismantle or significantly alter its structure have been largely unsuccessful.

In conclusion, the establishment of the Federal Reserve marked a significant shift in power dynamics, particularly in terms of veto power. The American people, who once had the ability to directly influence government decisions, saw their power diminished as the central bank gained control over monetary policy. While presidents like JFK and Andrew Jackson expressed opposition to the Federal Reserve, their efforts to challenge its authority were met with limited success. Understanding the significance of veto power and the consequences of its loss is crucial in comprehending the broader implications of the Federal Reserve's role in the American economy.

2.3 The Loss of Power After the Federal Reserve

The establishment of the Federal Reserve marked a significant shift in the power dynamics between the American people and the government. Before the creation of the Federal Reserve, the American people had certain powers, including the ability to exercise veto power, that allowed them to have a direct influence on government decisions. However, with the advent of the Federal Reserve, some of these powers were diminished, leading to a loss of control and influence over the nation's monetary and economic policies.

The American People's Power Before the Federal Reserve

Before the Federal Reserve, the American people had a more direct say in the nation's financial affairs. The Constitution granted Congress the power to coin money and regulate its value, ensuring that decisions regarding the nation's currency were made by elected representatives. This system provided a level of transparency and accountability, as the American people could hold their elected officials responsible for their monetary policies.

Additionally, the American people had a form of veto power through their elected representatives. If the government proposed policies or legislation that the people disagreed with, they could voice their concerns to their representatives, who had the power to vote against such measures. This system allowed for a more direct connection between the people and their government, ensuring that their voices were heard and their interests were represented.

The Loss of Power After the Federal Reserve

The creation of the Federal Reserve brought about a significant loss of power for the American people. The Federal Reserve Act of 1913 granted the newly established central bank the authority to control the nation's monetary policy, including the issuance of currency, setting interest rates, and regulating the banking system. This transfer of power from elected officials to an independent entity meant that decisions regarding the nation's economy were no longer directly influenced by the American people.

One of the key aspects of the loss of power was the removal of the American people's ability to exercise veto power over monetary policies. The Federal Reserve, being an independent entity, was not subject to direct control or oversight by elected officials. This meant that decisions made by the Federal Reserve, such as interest rate adjustments or quantitative easing measures, were not subject to the same level of scrutiny and accountability as decisions made by elected representatives.

Furthermore, the Federal Reserve's structure, with its regional banks and board of governors, created a level of insulation from public pressure. The board members of the Federal Reserve were appointed rather than elected, further distancing the decision-making process from the American people. This lack of direct accountability and transparency led to a loss of control over the nation's monetary policies and economic stability.

Presidential Opposition to the Federal Reserve

John F. Kennedy (JFK) was not the only president to express opposition to the Federal Reserve. Throughout history, several presidents have voiced concerns about the central bank's power and influence. For example, President Andrew Jackson was a staunch critic of central banking and vetoed the rechartering of the Second Bank of the United States in 1832. His opposition to the central bank was rooted in his belief that it concentrated too much power in the hands of a few, leading to corruption and economic inequality.

President Woodrow Wilson, who signed the Federal Reserve Act into law, later expressed regret over the consequences of its creation. He acknowledged that the Federal Reserve had become dominated by powerful banking interests and had not achieved its intended purpose of preventing financial crises.

Other presidents, such as Franklin D. Roosevelt and Richard Nixon, also had conflicts with the Federal Reserve. Roosevelt sought to exert more control over the central bank during the Great Depression, while Nixon clashed with the Federal Reserve over its monetary policy decisions during his presidency.

Outcomes of Presidential Opposition

Despite the opposition expressed by various presidents, the Federal Reserve has remained intact and largely independent. The central bank's influence and power have continued to grow over the years, with its decisions impacting the nation's economy and financial stability.

Presidential opposition to the Federal Reserve has often been met with resistance from the banking and financial sectors, as well as from within the Federal Reserve itself. The central bank's autonomy and insulation from political pressure have allowed it to withstand attempts to curtail its power or influence.

While some presidents have managed to influence the Federal Reserve's policies to some extent, such as through the appointment of sympathetic board members, the overall power dynamics between the American people and the central bank have not significantly shifted. The Federal Reserve remains a powerful institution with a considerable degree of control over the nation's monetary and economic policies.

In the next chapter, we will explore the influence of the Federal Reserve on the economy, including its role in shaping monetary policy, managing inflation and deflation, and its response to economic crises. Understanding these dynamics is crucial to comprehending the full impact of the Federal Reserve on the American people and the broader global economy.

Presidential Opposition to the Federal Reserve

3.1 JFK and his Attempt to End the Federal Reserve

President John F. Kennedy, often referred to as JFK, is known for his bold and controversial decisions during his presidency. One of the most significant actions he took was his attempt to end the Federal Reserve. Kennedy's opposition to the Federal Reserve stemmed from his belief that it wielded too much power and influence over the American economy, and that it needed to be reined in for the benefit of the American people.

Kennedy's skepticism towards the Federal Reserve was not unfounded. He believed that the central bank's policies, particularly its control over interest rates and the money supply, were detrimental to the economy and hindered the government's ability to implement effective fiscal policies. He saw the Federal Reserve as an unelected body that held immense power over the nation's financial system, and he sought to challenge its authority.

In 1963, Kennedy signed Executive Order 11110, which aimed to strip the Federal Reserve of its power to issue currency. The order authorized the Treasury Department to issue silver certificates, effectively bypassing the Federal Reserve's control over the money supply. Kennedy's intention was to reduce the influence of the central bank and restore the government's authority in monetary policy.

However, Kennedy's attempt to curtail the Federal Reserve's power was short-lived. Just a few months after signing the executive order, Kennedy was assassinated in Dallas, Texas, on November 22, 1963. His untimely death left his efforts to reform the Federal Reserve unfinished, and subsequent administrations did not pursue his agenda.

The outcome of Kennedy's opposition to the Federal Reserve was therefore inconclusive. While his executive order signaled a clear intent to challenge the central bank's authority, his assassination prevented any further progress in his mission. It is worth noting that the executive order itself did not explicitly aim to abolish the Federal Reserve but rather sought to limit its influence by empowering the Treasury Department.

Despite the lack of immediate success, Kennedy's actions sparked a broader conversation about the role and power of the Federal Reserve. His opposition to the central bank resonated with those who shared his concerns about its influence on the economy. Kennedy's attempt to end the Federal Reserve highlighted the need for a critical examination of the central bank's operations and its impact on the American people.

It is important to note that Kennedy was not the only president who expressed skepticism towards the Federal Reserve. Throughout history, several other presidents have voiced concerns about the central bank's power and influence. For example, President Woodrow Wilson, who signed the Federal Reserve Act into law in 1913, later expressed regret over the consequences of its creation. President Franklin D. Roosevelt also had reservations about the Federal Reserve's policies during the Great Depression.

However, despite these reservations, no president since Kennedy has made a concerted effort to dismantle or significantly reform the Federal Reserve. The central bank has remained a powerful institution, largely insulated from political interference. While presidents may express their concerns about the Federal Reserve, the institution's independence and the complexities of the financial system make it difficult to enact substantial changes without broad consensus and support.

In conclusion, JFK's attempt to end the Federal Reserve through Executive Order 11110 was a significant moment in the history of the central bank. Although his efforts were cut short by his assassination, his actions sparked a broader conversation about the power and influence of the Federal Reserve. While subsequent presidents have expressed reservations about the central bank, no significant reforms have been enacted since Kennedy's time. The Federal Reserve continues to play a crucial role in the American economy, and its influence remains a topic of debate and scrutiny.

3.2 Other Presidents' Efforts to Challenge the Federal Reserve

While President John F. Kennedy's opposition to the Federal Reserve is well-known, he was not the only president to challenge the institution. Throughout history, several other presidents have expressed concerns about the Federal Reserve's power and influence over the economy. These presidents sought to either reform or abolish the Federal Reserve, but their efforts were met with varying degrees of success and resistance.

One notable president who opposed the Federal Reserve was Andrew Jackson. Jackson, who served as the seventh president of the United States from 1829 to 1837, was a staunch advocate for limited government and believed that the central bank was an unconstitutional and undemocratic institution. He famously vetoed the rechartering of the Second Bank of the United States, which was the precursor to the Federal Reserve. Jackson argued that the bank favored the wealthy elite and had too much control over the nation's finances. Despite facing significant opposition, Jackson's veto stood, and the Second Bank of the United States ceased to exist.

Another president who challenged the Federal Reserve was Woodrow Wilson. Wilson, who served as the 28th president of the United States from 1913 to 1921, signed the Federal Reserve Act into law in 1913. However, later in his presidency, Wilson expressed regret over the creation of the Federal Reserve and its impact on the economy. He believed that the Federal Reserve had become too powerful and that its actions were contributing to economic instability. Wilson's concerns were particularly heightened during World War I when the Federal Reserve's policies led to inflation and increased government debt. Despite his reservations, Wilson was unable to enact any significant reforms to the Federal Reserve during his presidency.

President Franklin D. Roosevelt also had a complicated relationship with the Federal Reserve. Roosevelt, who served as the 32nd president of the United States from 1933 to 1945, implemented several policies aimed at stabilizing the economy during the Great Depression. While he did not openly challenge the Federal Reserve, Roosevelt's New Deal programs and increased government intervention in the economy were seen by some as a way to circumvent the influence of the central bank. Roosevelt's policies, such as the creation of the Securities and Exchange Commission and the establishment of the Federal Deposit Insurance Corporation, aimed to regulate the financial industry and protect consumers. These actions were seen by some as an attempt to assert government control over the banking system, which could be interpreted as a challenge to the Federal Reserve's authority.

In more recent history, President Donald Trump has also expressed skepticism and criticism of the Federal Reserve. Trump, who served as the 45th president of the United States from 2017 to 2021, frequently criticized the Federal Reserve's monetary policy decisions, particularly regarding interest rates. He argued that the Federal Reserve's actions were hindering economic growth and that the institution was not acting in the best interest of the American people. Trump called for lower interest rates to stimulate economic activity and often voiced his desire for a more accommodative monetary policy. However, despite his vocal opposition, Trump was unable to significantly alter the course of the Federal Reserve's policies during his presidency.

The outcomes of presidential opposition to the Federal Reserve have varied throughout history. While some presidents, like Andrew Jackson, were successful in challenging the institution, others faced significant resistance and were unable to enact meaningful reforms. The Federal Reserve, as an independent entity, has a considerable degree of autonomy and is not easily influenced by presidential opposition alone. The institution's structure and the support it receives from the financial industry and other influential stakeholders make it difficult for presidents to dismantle or significantly alter its operations.

It is important to note that the Federal Reserve's role and influence over the economy have evolved over time, and presidential opposition to the institution is not a new phenomenon. The debates surrounding the Federal Reserve's power and its impact on the economy continue to shape discussions about monetary policy and financial regulation. As the United States moves forward, it is crucial to understand the historical context and the various perspectives on the Federal Reserve to inform future discussions and potential reforms.

3.3 Outcomes of Presidential Opposition

Throughout the history of the Federal Reserve, several presidents have expressed opposition to its existence and attempted to challenge its power. While John F. Kennedy is often cited as the most prominent president to challenge the Federal Reserve, he was not the only one. Other presidents, both before and after Kennedy, have also voiced their concerns and attempted to curtail the influence of the central bank. However, the outcomes of their opposition varied, and the Federal Reserve has largely remained intact.

Presidential Opposition Before JFK

Before John F. Kennedy, there were presidents who expressed skepticism and opposition to the Federal Reserve. One notable example is Woodrow Wilson, who signed the Federal Reserve Act into law in 1913 but later regretted his decision. Wilson believed that the Federal Reserve had become too powerful and had strayed from its original purpose. He expressed concerns about the concentration of power in the hands of a few individuals and the lack of democratic accountability within the central bank.

Another president who opposed the Federal Reserve was Franklin D. Roosevelt. During his presidency, Roosevelt sought to exert greater control over the central bank and limit its independence. He believed that the Federal Reserve's policies were hindering economic recovery during the Great Depression. Roosevelt attempted to pack the Supreme Court with justices who would be more sympathetic to his policies, including those related to the Federal Reserve. However, his efforts were met with significant opposition and ultimately failed.

JFK and his Attempt to End the Federal Reserve

John F. Kennedy's opposition to the Federal Reserve is perhaps the most well-known and controversial. Kennedy believed that the central bank had too much power and was not acting in the best interests of the American people. He sought to dismantle the Federal Reserve and return the power to the U.S. Treasury Department. Kennedy's efforts to challenge the Federal Reserve were part of a broader agenda to reform the monetary system and reduce the influence of private banks.

Kennedy took several steps to undermine the Federal Reserve's authority. He issued Executive Order 11110, which authorized the U.S. Treasury to issue silver certificates, bypassing the Federal Reserve's control over the money supply. This move was seen as a direct challenge to the central bank's monopoly on currency issuance. Additionally, Kennedy appointed officials to key positions within the Treasury Department who were critical of the Federal Reserve's policies.

However, Kennedy's opposition to the Federal Reserve was short-lived. His presidency was tragically cut short by his assassination in 1963, and his efforts to challenge the central bank were never fully realized. After his death, subsequent administrations did not continue his opposition to the Federal Reserve, and the central bank's power remained largely intact.

Other Presidents' Efforts to Challenge the Federal Reserve

While John F. Kennedy's opposition to the Federal Reserve is the most well-known, he was not the only president to express concerns about the central bank. Several other presidents have also voiced their opposition and attempted to challenge the Federal Reserve's authority.

One such president was Richard Nixon. In the early 1970s, Nixon sought to exert greater control over the Federal Reserve and influence its monetary policy decisions. He believed that the central bank's policies were contributing to inflation and hindering economic growth. Nixon pressured the Federal Reserve to adopt expansionary monetary policies to stimulate the economy, but his efforts were met with resistance from the central bank.

Another president who challenged the Federal Reserve was Jimmy Carter. During his presidency in the late 1970s, Carter criticized the central bank for its handling of inflation and interest rates. He believed that the Federal Reserve's policies were contributing to economic instability and sought to exert greater control over its decision-making process. However, Carter's attempts to challenge the Federal Reserve were largely unsuccessful, and the central bank maintained its independence.

Outcomes of Presidential Opposition

The outcomes of presidential opposition to the Federal Reserve have varied throughout history. While some presidents, like John F. Kennedy, were able to take initial steps to challenge the central bank's authority, their efforts were often short-lived and did not result in significant changes to the Federal Reserve's structure or power.

The Federal Reserve, as an independent institution, has proven to be resilient and resistant to attempts to curtail its influence. The central bank's ability to control monetary policy and regulate the banking system has remained largely intact despite presidential opposition. While presidents may express their concerns and attempt to influence the Federal Reserve's policies, the central bank's autonomy and independence have allowed it to maintain its power and authority.

In conclusion, presidential opposition to the Federal Reserve has been a recurring theme throughout history. While some presidents, such as John F. Kennedy, have taken steps to challenge the central bank's authority, their efforts have often been met with resistance and have not resulted in significant changes to the Federal Reserve's power. The central bank's independence and autonomy have allowed it to withstand presidential opposition and maintain its influence over monetary policy and the banking system.

37

The Influence of the Federal Reserve on the Economy

4.1 Monetary Policy and its Impact

Monetary policy refers to the actions taken by a central bank, such as the Federal Reserve, to manage and control the money supply and interest rates in an economy. The Federal Reserve's monetary policy decisions have a significant impact on the overall economy, influencing factors such as inflation, employment, and economic growth. In this section, we will explore the concept of monetary policy and its various impacts.

The Role of the Federal Reserve in Monetary Policy

The Federal Reserve plays a crucial role in formulating and implementing monetary policy in the United States. Through its monetary policy tools, the Federal Reserve aims to achieve its dual mandate of promoting maximum employment and stable prices. The primary tool used by the Federal Reserve to influence monetary policy is the manipulation of interest rates.

Interest Rates and their Impact

Interest rates have a profound impact on the economy, affecting various sectors and individuals. When the Federal Reserve lowers interest rates, it becomes cheaper for businesses and individuals to borrow money. This stimulates investment and consumption, leading to increased economic activity and job creation. Lower interest rates also make it more attractive for businesses to invest in capital projects, such as expanding production facilities or purchasing new equipment.

Conversely, when the Federal Reserve raises interest rates, borrowing becomes more expensive, which can dampen economic activity. Higher interest rates make it less attractive for businesses and individuals to borrow, leading to reduced investment and consumption. This can slow down economic growth and potentially lead to a contraction in employment.

Inflation and Deflation

Another crucial aspect of monetary policy is its impact on inflation and deflation. Inflation refers to the general increase in prices over time, while deflation refers to a decrease in prices. The Federal Reserve aims to maintain price stability by keeping inflation in check.

To control inflation, the Federal Reserve can raise interest rates. By increasing borrowing costs, the Federal Reserve aims to reduce spending and curb inflationary pressures. Conversely, during periods of deflation or low inflation, the Federal Reserve may lower interest rates to stimulate spending and encourage economic growth.

The Federal Reserve's Role in Economic Crises

The Federal Reserve also plays a critical role in managing and mitigating economic crises. During times of financial instability or recession, the Federal Reserve can implement expansionary monetary policy measures to stimulate the economy. This can include lowering interest rates, providing liquidity to financial institutions, and implementing quantitative easing programs.

By injecting liquidity into the financial system, the Federal Reserve aims to stabilize markets, restore confidence, and encourage lending and investment. These measures can help prevent a severe economic downturn and support the recovery process.

However, the Federal Reserve's actions during economic crises have been a subject of debate and criticism. Some argue that the Federal Reserve's interventions can distort market mechanisms and create moral hazard, as financial institutions may take excessive risks knowing that the Federal Reserve will provide support in times of crisis. Others contend that the Federal Reserve's actions are necessary to prevent systemic collapse and protect the overall economy.

The Impact of Monetary Policy on Different Stakeholders

Monetary policy decisions by the Federal Reserve can have varying impacts on different stakeholders in the economy. For example, lower interest rates can benefit borrowers, such as businesses and individuals seeking loans for investment or consumption. On the other hand, savers may experience reduced returns on their savings due to lower interest rates.

Additionally, the impact of monetary policy can differ across industries and sectors. For instance, industries that are more sensitive to interest rates, such as housing and construction, may experience significant fluctuations in activity based on changes in monetary policy. Similarly, the stock market can be influenced by the Federal Reserve's actions, as investors assess the potential impact on corporate earnings and future economic conditions.

Conclusion

Monetary policy is a powerful tool used by the Federal Reserve to manage the economy and achieve its objectives of maximum employment and stable prices. Through the manipulation of interest rates, the Federal Reserve can influence borrowing costs, inflation, and economic activity. However, the impact of monetary policy can vary across different stakeholders and sectors of the economy. Understanding the intricacies of monetary policy is crucial for individuals, businesses, and policymakers to navigate the ever-changing economic landscape.

4.2 Inflation and Deflation

Inflation and deflation are two economic phenomena that have a significant impact on the stability and growth of an economy. These terms refer to the changes in the overall price level of goods and services in an economy over time. Understanding the causes and consequences of inflation and deflation is crucial in comprehending the role of the Federal Reserve in managing the economy.

Inflation is the sustained increase in the general price level of goods and services in an economy over a period of time. It erodes the purchasing power of money, as the same amount of currency can buy fewer goods and services. Inflation can be caused by various factors, including an increase in the money supply, higher production costs, or increased demand for goods and services. When inflation is moderate and predictable, it can have some positive effects, such as encouraging spending and investment. However, high or unpredictable inflation can lead to economic instability and negatively impact individuals and businesses.

The Federal Reserve plays a crucial role in managing inflation through its monetary policy tools. One of the primary tools used by the Federal Reserve to control inflation is **interest rates**. By adjusting the federal funds rate, which is the interest rate at which banks lend to each other, the Federal Reserve can influence borrowing costs for businesses and consumers. When the Federal Reserve wants to combat inflation, it may raise interest rates to reduce borrowing and spending, thereby slowing down economic activity and curbing price increases.

Deflation, on the other hand, is the sustained decrease in the general price level of goods and services in an economy. Deflation can occur due to factors such as a decrease in the money supply, lower production costs, or a decrease in demand for goods and services. While deflation may seem beneficial as it increases the purchasing power of money, it can have detrimental effects on the economy. Deflation can lead to a decrease in consumer spending and business investment, as individuals and businesses delay purchases in anticipation of lower prices in the future. This can result in a downward spiral of economic activity, known as a deflationary spiral, which can be difficult to reverse.

The Federal Reserve aims to maintain a stable inflation rate that is conducive to economic growth and stability. The Federal Open Market Committee (FOMC), the monetary policymaking body within the Federal Reserve, sets an inflation target of around 2 percent. This target is based on the belief that a moderate level of inflation can support economic growth and prevent the harmful effects of deflation.

The Federal Reserve utilizes various tools to manage inflation and deflation. In addition to adjusting interest rates, the Federal Reserve can also engage in **open market operations**. This involves buying or selling government securities in the open market to influence the money supply and interest rates. By purchasing government securities, the Federal Reserve injects money into the economy, increasing the money supply and potentially stimulating economic activity. Conversely, selling government securities reduces the money supply, which can help control inflationary pressures.

It is important to note that the Federal Reserve's ability to manage inflation and deflation is not without challenges. Economic conditions and external factors can complicate the Federal Reserve's efforts to maintain price stability. For example, global economic events, such as changes in oil prices or shifts in international trade, can impact inflation rates in the United States. Additionally, accurately predicting and responding to inflationary or deflationary pressures requires a deep understanding of the complex dynamics of the economy.

In conclusion, inflation and deflation are significant economic phenomena that impact the stability and growth of an economy. The Federal Reserve plays a crucial role in managing these phenomena through its monetary policy tools, such as adjusting interest rates and engaging in open market operations. By striving to maintain a stable inflation rate, the Federal Reserve aims to support economic growth and stability. However, managing inflation and deflation is a complex task that requires careful analysis of economic conditions and external factors.

4.3 Interest Rates and the Federal Reserve

Interest rates play a crucial role in the functioning of the economy, and the Federal Reserve has significant influence over them. In this section, we will explore the relationship between interest rates and the Federal Reserve, and how its decisions impact the economy.

The Federal Reserve, as the central bank of the United States, has the authority to set and adjust interest rates. It does so through its monetary policy tools, primarily by manipulating the federal funds rate. The federal funds rate is the interest rate at which banks lend to each other overnight to meet reserve requirements. Changes in this rate have a ripple effect throughout the economy, influencing borrowing costs, investment decisions, and overall economic activity.

One of the primary objectives of the Federal Reserve is to maintain price stability and promote maximum employment. To achieve these goals, it utilizes interest rate adjustments as a tool to manage inflation and stimulate or cool down economic growth.

When the Federal Reserve wants to stimulate economic activity, it lowers interest rates. By reducing borrowing costs, it encourages businesses and individuals to take on more debt, invest, and spend. This increased economic activity can lead to job creation and higher consumer spending, ultimately boosting economic growth.

Conversely, when the Federal Reserve wants to curb inflation or slow down an overheating economy, it raises interest rates. Higher interest rates make borrowing more expensive, which can discourage businesses and individuals from taking on new debt. This can help reduce spending and cool down the economy, potentially preventing excessive inflationary pressures.

The Federal Reserve's decisions regarding interest rates are made by the Federal Open Market Committee (FOMC), which consists of the seven members of the Board of Governors and five Reserve Bank presidents. The FOMC meets regularly to assess economic conditions and determine the appropriate course of action regarding interest rates.

It is important to note that the Federal Reserve's influence over interest rates is not absolute. Market forces and other factors also play a role in determining interest rates. However, the Federal Reserve's actions can have a significant impact on market expectations and investor behavior, which in turn can influence interest rates.

The Federal Reserve's control over interest rates has both benefits and drawbacks. On the positive side, it allows the central bank to respond to changing economic conditions and steer the economy in the desired direction. By adjusting interest rates, the Federal Reserve can help stabilize the economy during periods of recession or inflationary pressures.

However, the Federal Reserve's power over interest rates also raises concerns. Critics argue that the central bank's decisions can have unintended consequences and distort market signals. They argue that artificially low interest rates, for example, can encourage excessive risk-taking and asset bubbles, while high interest rates can stifle economic growth and hinder investment.

Furthermore, the Federal Reserve's influence over interest rates has been a subject of controversy and debate. Some argue that the central bank's decisions are influenced by political considerations or the interests of powerful financial institutions. This has led to calls for greater transparency and accountability in the Federal Reserve's decision-making process.

In recent years, the Federal Reserve has faced challenges in managing interest rates due to the prolonged period of low inflation and low-interest rates. This has limited the central bank's ability to use interest rate adjustments as a tool for stimulating the economy during downturns.

To address this, the Federal Reserve has explored unconventional monetary policy measures, such as quantitative easing, to provide additional stimulus to the economy. These measures involve the purchase of government bonds and other securities to inject liquidity into the financial system and lower long-term interest rates.

In conclusion, interest rates are a critical tool in the Federal Reserve's arsenal for managing the economy. The central bank's decisions regarding interest rates have far-reaching implications for borrowing costs, investment, and overall economic activity. While the Federal Reserve's control over interest rates allows it to respond to economic conditions, it also raises concerns about market distortions and the need for transparency and accountability. Understanding the relationship between interest rates and the Federal Reserve is essential for comprehending the broader impact of its policies on the economy.

4.4 The Federal Reserve's Role in Economic Crises

The Federal Reserve, as the central bank of the United States, plays a significant role in managing the country's economy. One crucial aspect of its responsibilities is its role in addressing and mitigating economic crises. Throughout its history, the Federal Reserve has faced numerous economic downturns and financial crises, and its actions during these periods have had a profound impact on the nation's economy.

One of the most notable economic crises in U.S. history was the Great Depression, which began with the stock market crash of 1929. The Federal Reserve's response to this crisis has been a subject of debate and analysis for decades. Some critics argue that the Federal Reserve's tight monetary policy in the years leading up to the crash contributed to the severity of the Depression. By restricting the money supply and raising interest rates, the Federal Reserve inadvertently worsened the economic downturn, leading to bank failures, unemployment, and a prolonged period of economic hardship.

In response to the Great Depression, the Federal Reserve implemented various measures to stabilize the economy. It lowered interest rates, injected liquidity into the banking system, and implemented policies to restore confidence in the financial sector. These actions, along with other government interventions such as the New Deal, helped to alleviate some of the economic distress caused by the Depression. However, it is important to note that the Federal Reserve's role in the crisis remains a subject of ongoing debate among economists and historians.

Another significant economic crisis that tested the Federal Reserve's ability to manage the economy was the financial crisis of 2008. This crisis, often referred to as the Great Recession, was triggered by the collapse of the housing market and the subsequent failure of major financial institutions. The Federal Reserve played a crucial role in responding to this crisis and preventing a complete collapse of the financial system.

During the crisis, the Federal Reserve implemented a range of unconventional monetary policy measures to stabilize the economy. It lowered interest rates to near-zero levels and engaged in large-scale asset purchases, a policy known as quantitative easing. These measures were aimed at stimulating economic growth, increasing liquidity in the financial system, and preventing a deflationary spiral.

The Federal Reserve also worked closely with other government agencies, such as the Treasury Department, to implement various programs to support the financial sector and provide assistance to struggling homeowners. These efforts included the Troubled Asset Relief Program (TARP) and the Home Affordable Modification Program (HAMP).

While the Federal Reserve's actions during the 2008 financial crisis were generally seen as necessary to prevent a complete economic collapse, they were not without controversy. Critics argue that the Federal Reserve's interventions, particularly its quantitative easing programs, have contributed to income inequality, inflated asset prices, and created a moral hazard by bailing out large financial institutions.

It is important to note that the Federal Reserve's role in economic crises extends beyond its response to specific events. The central bank also plays a crucial role in monitoring and assessing potential risks to the economy and implementing policies to prevent or mitigate future crises. This includes conducting regular economic and financial market analysis, supervising and regulating financial institutions, and implementing macroprudential policies to promote financial stability.

In conclusion, the Federal Reserve's role in economic crises is multifaceted and complex. While its actions during periods of crisis have been instrumental in stabilizing the economy and preventing further damage, they have also been subject to criticism and debate. The Federal Reserve's ability to effectively manage economic crises is an ongoing challenge that requires a delicate balance between promoting economic growth, maintaining financial stability, and addressing the concerns of various stakeholders.

Transparency and Accountability of the Federal Reserve

5.1 The Lack of Transparency

The lack of transparency surrounding the Federal Reserve has been a subject of concern and controversy since its inception. Critics argue that the central bank operates with a level of secrecy that is incompatible with a democratic society. This section will delve into the reasons behind the lack of transparency within the Federal Reserve and the implications it has for the American people.

One of the primary reasons for the lack of transparency is the Federal Reserve's unique structure and independence. Unlike other government agencies, the Federal Reserve is not subject to direct oversight by the executive, legislative, or judicial branches. It operates as an independent entity, making its own decisions regarding monetary policy and financial regulation. This independence was intentionally designed to insulate the central bank from political pressures and ensure its ability to make objective decisions in the best interest of the economy.

However, this independence also means that the Federal Reserve is not required to disclose its decision-making processes or the details of its operations to the public. While the Federal Reserve does release some information, such as meeting minutes and economic forecasts, critics argue that these disclosures are insufficient and lack the necessary level of transparency.

Another factor contributing to the lack of transparency is the complex nature of the Federal Reserve's operations. The central bank engages in a wide range of activities, including setting interest rates, conducting open market operations, and supervising and regulating banks. These activities involve intricate financial mechanisms and require a deep understanding of monetary policy and economics. As a result, the Federal Reserve's actions can be difficult for the average citizen to comprehend, making it challenging for the public to hold the institution accountable.

The lack of transparency within the Federal Reserve has significant implications for the American people. Without access to comprehensive information about the central bank's decision-making processes, it becomes difficult for individuals and organizations to assess the Federal Reserve's actions and hold it accountable for its policies. This lack of accountability can erode public trust in the institution and undermine its legitimacy.

Furthermore, the lack of transparency can lead to a perception of favoritism or bias in the Federal Reserve's operations. Critics argue that the central bank's close relationships with large financial institutions and its role in bailing out troubled banks during times of crisis create a perception that the Federal Reserve prioritizes the interests of Wall Street over those of Main Street. This perception further fuels distrust and skepticism towards the institution.

Efforts to increase transparency within the Federal Reserve have been met with mixed results. In recent years, there have been calls for greater disclosure of the central bank's decision-making processes, including demands for a full audit of the Federal Reserve. Advocates argue that increased transparency would enhance public trust and allow for a more informed public debate about the institution's policies.

However, opponents of increased transparency argue that it could compromise the Federal Reserve's independence and effectiveness. They contend that public scrutiny and political pressure could lead to short-term decision-making and undermine the central bank's ability to make objective, long-term decisions in the best interest of the economy.

In conclusion, the lack of transparency within the Federal Reserve is a contentious issue that has sparked debates about the institution's accountability and legitimacy. While the central bank's independence and complex operations contribute to the lack of transparency, critics argue that greater disclosure is necessary to ensure public trust and hold the Federal Reserve accountable for its policies. Balancing the need for transparency with the central bank's independence remains a challenge, but it is a crucial step towards fostering a more informed and engaged citizenry.

5.2 Auditing the Federal Reserve

The Federal Reserve, as a central bank, wields significant power over the American economy. Given its immense influence, it is crucial to ensure transparency and accountability in its operations. One way to achieve this is through auditing the Federal Reserve.

The Need for Auditing

Auditing is a process of examining and evaluating an organization's financial records, transactions, and operations to ensure accuracy, legality, and adherence to established standards. It provides an independent and objective assessment of an institution's financial health and performance.

The Federal Reserve, being responsible for monetary policy, regulating banks, and maintaining financial stability, should be subject to regular audits. Auditing the Federal Reserve is essential to ensure that it operates in the best interest of the American people and remains accountable for its actions.

The Current State of Auditing

Historically, the Federal Reserve has been resistant to external audits. It has argued that such audits would compromise its independence and hinder its ability to make effective monetary policy decisions. However, this lack of transparency has raised concerns among critics who believe that the Federal Reserve should be subject to the same level of scrutiny as other government agencies.

Currently, the Government Accountability Office (GAO) is authorized to conduct limited audits of the Federal Reserve. However, these audits are primarily focused on financial statements and do not provide a comprehensive examination of the Federal Reserve's activities. The GAO is prohibited from auditing certain areas, such as monetary policy decisions and transactions with foreign central banks.

Calls for Increased Auditing

In recent years, there have been growing calls for increased auditing of the Federal Reserve. Advocates argue that greater transparency and accountability are necessary to ensure the Federal Reserve's actions align with the best interests of the American people.

One proposed solution is the Federal Reserve Transparency Act, also known as the Audit the Fed bill. This legislation, introduced multiple times in Congress, seeks to expand the scope of audits conducted by the GAO. It aims to remove the restrictions on auditing monetary policy decisions and transactions with foreign central banks.

Proponents of the Audit the Fed bill argue that a comprehensive audit would shed light on the Federal Reserve's decision-making process, its impact on the economy, and potential conflicts of interest. They believe that increased transparency would help restore public trust in the institution and ensure that it remains accountable to the American people.

Opposition and Challenges

Despite the calls for increased auditing, there has been significant opposition to the idea. Critics argue that subjecting the Federal Reserve to extensive audits could undermine its independence and politicize its decision-making process. They contend that the Federal Reserve's ability to act swiftly and effectively during times of economic crisis could be compromised if it is constantly under scrutiny.

Additionally, opponents argue that auditing monetary policy decisions could lead to market instability. They believe that public disclosure of sensitive information could create uncertainty and potentially harm the economy.

Finding a Balance

The debate surrounding auditing the Federal Reserve revolves around finding a balance between transparency and independence. While it is crucial to ensure accountability, it is equally important to safeguard the Federal Reserve's ability to make informed and unbiased decisions.

One potential solution is to establish a framework for auditing that strikes a balance between transparency and independence. This could involve conducting regular audits of the Federal Reserve's financial statements while maintaining restrictions on auditing specific areas, such as monetary policy decisions.

By implementing a comprehensive auditing process, the Federal Reserve can address concerns regarding its transparency and accountability. It would provide the American people with a clearer understanding of the institution's operations and decision-making, fostering trust and confidence in its actions.

In conclusion, auditing the Federal Reserve is essential to ensure transparency and accountability. While there are valid concerns regarding the potential impact on independence and market stability, finding a balance between these factors is crucial. By establishing a framework for comprehensive audits, the Federal Reserve can address these concerns and enhance public trust in its operations.

5.3 Calls for Increased Accountability

The Federal Reserve, as an institution, has long been criticized for its lack of transparency and accountability. Many individuals and organizations have called for increased oversight and scrutiny of the Federal Reserve's actions and decision-making processes. These calls for accountability stem from concerns about the concentration of power within the institution and the potential for abuse or manipulation.

One of the primary concerns raised by critics is the lack of transparency surrounding the Federal Reserve's operations. Unlike other government agencies, the Federal Reserve is not subject to regular audits or public scrutiny. This lack of transparency has led to suspicions and conspiracy theories about the institution's true motives and actions. Critics argue that without proper oversight, the Federal Reserve can operate without accountability, potentially making decisions that benefit a select few at the expense of the broader public.

In recent years, there have been increasing calls for the Federal Reserve to be audited. Advocates for auditing the Federal Reserve argue that it is essential to understand the institution's decision-making processes and the impact of its policies on the economy. They believe that a comprehensive audit would shed light on the Federal Reserve's operations, including its lending practices, relationships with financial institutions, and the extent of its influence over the economy.

Efforts to increase accountability have gained traction in Congress, with several bills introduced to audit the Federal Reserve. One notable example is the Federal Reserve Transparency Act, also known as the Audit the Fed bill. This bill, introduced multiple times in Congress, seeks to subject the Federal Reserve to a full audit by the Government Accountability Office (GAO). Supporters of the bill argue that increased transparency would help restore public trust in the institution and ensure that it operates in the best interest of the American people.

However, despite these calls for increased accountability, the Federal Reserve has resisted efforts to subject it to a comprehensive audit. The institution argues that such audits would compromise its independence and hinder its ability to make effective monetary policy decisions. The Federal Reserve maintains that it already provides a significant amount of information to the public through its regular reports and statements and that subjecting it to additional audits would be unnecessary and potentially harmful.

In addition to calls for auditing, there have been proposals to increase the accountability of the Federal Reserve through other means. Some advocates argue for greater congressional oversight of the institution, including regular hearings and questioning of Federal Reserve officials. They believe that increased scrutiny would help ensure that the Federal Reserve remains accountable to the American people and that its actions align with the public interest.

Furthermore, there have been discussions about the composition of the Federal Reserve's decision-making bodies, such as the Federal Open Market Committee (FOMC). Critics argue that the current structure of the FOMC, which includes both appointed officials and regional bank presidents, may lead to conflicts of interest and a lack of diversity in perspectives. They propose reforms that would make the decision-making process more transparent and inclusive, potentially by including representatives from a broader range of stakeholders.

Overall, the calls for increased accountability of the Federal Reserve reflect a desire for greater transparency and oversight of an institution that wields significant power over the economy. Advocates argue that increased accountability would help ensure that the Federal Reserve operates in the best interest of the American people and that its decisions are based on sound economic principles rather than the interests of a select few. While efforts to increase accountability have faced resistance, the ongoing discussions and debates surrounding the Federal Reserve's role and operations indicate a growing recognition of the need for greater transparency and oversight.

The Federal Reserve and the Banking System

6.1 The Relationship Between the Federal Reserve and Banks

The relationship between the Federal Reserve and banks is a complex and intertwined one. To fully understand this relationship, it is important to delve into the history and functions of the Federal Reserve System, as well as the role of banks in the economy.

The Federal Reserve System, often referred to as the Fed, was established in 1913 with the primary purpose of providing stability to the nation's financial system. It was created in response to a series of financial panics and economic crises that plagued the United States in the late 19th and early 20th centuries. One of the key motivations behind its creation was to centralize control over the nation's monetary policy and banking system.

At its core, the Federal Reserve acts as the central bank of the United States. It is responsible for regulating and supervising banks, implementing monetary policy, and maintaining the stability of the financial system. The Federal Reserve achieves these objectives through various mechanisms, such as setting interest rates, controlling the money supply, and providing liquidity to banks.

Banks, on the other hand, play a crucial role in the economy by facilitating the flow of funds between savers and borrowers. They accept deposits from individuals and businesses and use those funds to provide loans and credit. Banks also serve as intermediaries in the payment system, enabling the smooth functioning of transactions.

The relationship between the Federal Reserve and banks can be understood through the lens of regulation and control. The Federal Reserve has the authority to regulate and supervise banks to ensure their safety and soundness. This includes setting capital requirements, conducting regular examinations, and enforcing compliance with banking laws and regulations.

Furthermore, the Federal Reserve has the power to influence the lending activities of banks through its monetary policy tools. By adjusting interest rates and controlling the money supply, the Federal Reserve can encourage or discourage lending and borrowing. This, in turn, affects the availability of credit in the economy and can have a significant impact on economic growth and stability.

The Federal Reserve also acts as a lender of last resort to banks. In times of financial stress or liquidity shortages, banks can borrow funds from the Federal Reserve through various lending facilities. This helps to ensure the stability of the banking system and prevent widespread bank failures.

While the Federal Reserve has significant control and influence over the banking system, it is important to note that banks are not entirely subservient to the Federal Reserve. Banks operate as independent entities and make their own lending decisions based on a variety of factors, including risk assessment, profitability, and market conditions. The Federal Reserve's role is to provide a regulatory framework and set the overall monetary policy direction, but it does not dictate the day-to-day operations of individual banks.

In terms of the power dynamics before and after the establishment of the Federal Reserve, there were notable changes. Before the Federal Reserve, the American people had limited control over the government's monetary policy. The banking system was largely decentralized, with numerous private banks issuing their own currency. This lack of centralization and regulation led to frequent financial panics and economic instability.

With the creation of the Federal Reserve, the power to control monetary policy and regulate the banking system was consolidated in the hands of a centralized authority. This shift meant that the American people had less direct influence over the government's monetary decisions. While the Federal Reserve is accountable to Congress and subject to oversight, its decision-making processes are often complex and opaque, making it challenging for the average citizen to fully understand or influence its actions.

In terms of presidential opposition to the Federal Reserve, John F. Kennedy (JFK) is often cited as a prominent example. JFK was critical of the Federal Reserve's policies and sought to curtail its power. He reportedly issued an executive order in 1963, known as Executive Order 11110, which aimed to transfer the authority to issue currency from the Federal Reserve to the Treasury Department. However, JFK's efforts were cut short by his assassination later that year, and the executive order was never fully implemented.

Other presidents, such as Andrew Jackson and Woodrow Wilson, also expressed concerns about the concentration of power in the hands of the Federal Reserve. However, their opposition did not result in significant changes to the structure or operations of the Federal Reserve.

In conclusion, the relationship between the Federal Reserve and banks is one of regulation, control, and interdependence. The Federal Reserve plays a crucial role in overseeing and influencing the activities of banks, while banks serve as intermediaries in the economy. The establishment of the Federal Reserve brought about a shift in power dynamics, reducing the direct influence of the American people over monetary policy decisions. While there have been instances of presidential opposition to the Federal Reserve, significant changes to its structure or operations have been limited.

6.2 Banking Regulations and the Federal Reserve

The Federal Reserve, as the central banking system of the United States, plays a crucial role in regulating and overseeing the country's banking industry. Through its various regulations, the Federal Reserve aims to maintain stability, promote economic growth, and protect the interests of both consumers and financial institutions. In this section, we will explore the banking regulations implemented by the Federal Reserve and their impact on the banking system.

The Evolution of Banking Regulations

Banking regulations in the United States have evolved significantly over time, with the establishment of the Federal Reserve marking a turning point in the regulatory landscape. Prior to the creation of the Federal Reserve in 1913, banking regulations were primarily the responsibility of individual states. This decentralized approach led to a lack of uniformity and consistency in banking practices across the country.

With the establishment of the Federal Reserve, a more centralized and comprehensive regulatory framework was put in place. The Federal Reserve Act granted the Federal Reserve the authority to regulate and supervise banks, ensuring their safety and soundness. This included the power to set reserve requirements, conduct examinations, and establish rules for banking operations.

The Role of the Federal Reserve in Banking Regulations

One of the key responsibilities of the Federal Reserve is to establish and enforce regulations that govern the banking industry. These regulations are designed to promote stability, protect consumers, and prevent financial crises. Some of the key areas covered by these regulations include:

Capital Requirements

The Federal Reserve sets minimum capital requirements for banks, which serve as a buffer against potential losses. These requirements ensure that banks maintain a sufficient level of capital to absorb losses and continue operating even during times of financial stress. By enforcing capital requirements, the Federal Reserve aims to enhance the resilience of the banking system and protect depositors' funds.

Liquidity Requirements

In addition to capital requirements, the Federal Reserve also establishes liquidity requirements for banks. These requirements ensure that banks have enough liquid assets to meet their short-term obligations and withstand liquidity shocks. By maintaining adequate liquidity, banks can fulfill their role as intermediaries in the economy and provide credit to businesses and individuals.

Consumer Protection

The Federal Reserve plays a vital role in protecting consumers in their interactions with banks. It enforces regulations such as the Truth in Lending Act, which requires banks to disclose the terms and costs of credit to consumers. Additionally, the Federal Reserve oversees compliance with regulations related to fair lending practices, ensuring that banks do not engage in discriminatory lending practices.

Anti-Money Laundering and Counter-Terrorism Financing

The Federal Reserve, along with other regulatory agencies, enforces regulations aimed at combating money laundering and the financing of terrorism. Banks are required to implement robust anti-money laundering (AML) programs and report suspicious transactions to the appropriate authorities. These regulations help prevent illicit funds from entering the financial system and contribute to national security efforts.

The Impact of Banking Regulations

Banking regulations implemented by the Federal Reserve have had a significant impact on the banking system and the broader economy. While regulations aim to promote stability and protect consumers, they can also impose costs on financial institutions and potentially limit their ability to generate profits. Striking the right balance between regulation and innovation is a constant challenge for policymakers.

On one hand, banking regulations have helped prevent financial crises by imposing stricter capital and liquidity requirements on banks. These regulations have made the banking system more resilient and better equipped to withstand economic shocks. By promoting stability, the Federal Reserve's regulations contribute to a more secure financial environment for both banks and their customers.

On the other hand, some argue that excessive regulations can stifle innovation and hinder economic growth. Critics argue that stringent regulations may discourage banks from taking risks and lending to certain sectors of the economy. Striking the right balance between regulation and allowing for innovation and growth is an ongoing challenge for policymakers.

In conclusion, the Federal Reserve plays a crucial role in regulating the banking industry through the implementation of various banking regulations. These regulations aim to promote stability, protect consumers, and prevent financial crises. While regulations have undoubtedly made the banking system more resilient, finding the right balance between regulation and innovation remains an ongoing challenge. By understanding the role of banking regulations and their impact, individuals can gain a deeper insight into the functioning of the Federal Reserve and its influence on the banking system.

6.3 The Federal Reserve's Control Over the Banking System

The establishment of the Federal Reserve brought about a significant shift in the power dynamics between the American people and the government, particularly in relation to the banking system. Before delving into the control the Federal Reserve holds over the banking system, it is crucial to understand the power the American people had over the government before its creation and the subsequent loss of power after its establishment.

The American People's Power Before the Federal Reserve

Prior to the creation of the Federal Reserve, the American people held a certain level of power over the government, particularly through their ability to influence legislation and policy decisions. One of the key powers they possessed was the ability to exercise their voice through the democratic process, primarily through voting for representatives who would advocate for their interests.

Additionally, the American people had a form of indirect power through the system of checks and balances, which included the power of veto. The president, as the head of the executive branch, had the authority to veto legislation passed by Congress if they believed it was not in the best interest of the American people. This power acted as a safeguard against policies that could potentially harm the nation's economy or infringe upon individual rights.

The Loss of Power After the Federal Reserve

With the establishment of the Federal Reserve in 1913, the power dynamics between the American people and the government underwent a significant transformation. The Federal Reserve, as a central banking system, was granted substantial control over the nation's monetary policy and banking system. This shift in power resulted in a diminished influence of the American people over economic decisions and the financial sector.

One of the key aspects that contributed to the loss of power was the centralization of monetary policy. The Federal Reserve was given the authority to control the money supply, set interest rates, and regulate banks. This consolidation of power effectively removed the American people's ability to directly influence these crucial economic decisions.

Furthermore, the Federal Reserve's independence from direct political control meant that its policies and actions were not subject to the same level of scrutiny and accountability as other government agencies. This lack of transparency further limited the American people's ability to hold the Federal Reserve accountable for its decisions and actions.

Presidential Opposition to the Federal Reserve

John F. Kennedy (JFK) was one of the notable presidents who expressed opposition to the Federal Reserve and made efforts to challenge its authority. In the early 1960s, JFK sought to curtail the power of the Federal Reserve by issuing Executive Order 11110, which aimed to transfer the authority to issue currency from the Federal Reserve to the United States Department of the Treasury. This move was seen as an attempt to regain control over the nation's monetary policy and reduce the influence of the Federal Reserve.

However, JFK's efforts to challenge the Federal Reserve were short-lived, as he was assassinated in 1963, leaving his proposed reforms unfinished. It is worth noting that the exact motivations behind JFK's opposition to the Federal Reserve remain a subject of debate and speculation.

Other presidents, such as Andrew Jackson and Woodrow Wilson, also expressed concerns about the concentration of power in the hands of the banking elite and the potential influence of central banks. However, their opposition did not result in significant changes to the Federal Reserve's structure or authority.

Outcomes of Presidential Opposition

The opposition of presidents to the Federal Reserve has had limited success in challenging its authority or bringing about substantial reforms. While some presidents, like JFK, made attempts to curtail the power of the Federal Reserve, their efforts were often met with resistance and ultimately did not lead to significant changes in the Federal Reserve's control over the banking system.

The Federal Reserve, as an independent entity, has continued to exert its influence over monetary policy and banking regulations. Its decisions and actions have had far-reaching implications for the American economy and the global financial system.

In conclusion, the establishment of the Federal Reserve resulted in a significant shift in power dynamics between the American people and the government, particularly in relation to the banking system. The American people's power, including their ability to exercise veto power and influence legislation, was diminished after the creation of the Federal Reserve. While some presidents, including JFK, expressed opposition to the Federal Reserve, their efforts to challenge its authority had limited success. The Federal Reserve's control over the banking system remains a contentious issue, with ongoing debates about its transparency, accountability, and the need for reforms.

The Federal Reserve and the Global Economy

7.1 The Federal Reserve's Role in the Global Financial System

The Federal Reserve, as the central bank of the United States, plays a significant role not only in the domestic economy but also in the global financial system. Its actions and policies have far-reaching implications that extend beyond national borders. In this section, we will explore the Federal Reserve's role in the global financial system, its influence on international monetary policy, and the impacts of its actions on global markets.

The Federal Reserve's primary mandate is to promote price stability, maximum employment, and moderate long-term interest rates within the United States. However, due to the interconnectedness of the global economy, the Federal Reserve's decisions and policies have a profound impact on the international financial landscape.

One of the key ways in which the Federal Reserve influences the global financial system is through its monetary policy. The Federal Reserve has the power to adjust interest rates, control the money supply, and conduct open market operations. These actions have a direct impact on the value of the U.S. dollar, which is the world's primary reserve currency. Changes in U.S. interest rates can attract or repel foreign investors, affecting capital flows and exchange rates in other countries.

Moreover, the Federal Reserve's monetary policy decisions can have spillover effects on other economies. For example, when the Federal Reserve raises interest rates, it can lead to a strengthening of the U.S. dollar. This, in turn, can make borrowing more expensive for countries that have borrowed in dollars, potentially causing financial stress and economic instability in those nations. Conversely, when the Federal Reserve lowers interest rates, it can stimulate borrowing and investment, not only in the United States but also in other countries.

The Federal Reserve also plays a crucial role in international monetary policy coordination. As a member of various international organizations, such as the International Monetary Fund (IMF) and the Bank for International Settlements (BIS), the Federal Reserve collaborates with other central banks to address global economic challenges. Through these forums, central bankers discuss and coordinate policies to maintain stability in the global financial system.

In times of financial crises, the Federal Reserve often takes a leading role in providing liquidity to global markets. For instance, during the 2008 financial crisis, the Federal Reserve implemented a series of unconventional measures, such as quantitative easing and currency swap lines, to stabilize financial markets and prevent a collapse of the global banking system. These actions not only benefited the United States but also had a positive impact on other countries by restoring confidence and preventing a deeper economic downturn.

However, the Federal Reserve's role in the global financial system is not without criticism. Some argue that the Federal Reserve's policies, particularly its monetary easing measures, can lead to unintended consequences and distortions in global markets. For example, the influx of liquidity resulting from quantitative easing can fuel asset bubbles in emerging markets and create imbalances in the global economy.

Additionally, the Federal Reserve's decisions can have a significant impact on commodity prices, particularly those denominated in U.S. dollars. As the value of the dollar fluctuates, it can affect the prices of commodities such as oil, gold, and agricultural products. These price fluctuations can have far-reaching consequences for commodity-exporting countries and global supply chains.

In recent years, there has been a growing recognition of the need for enhanced international cooperation and coordination in monetary policy. As the global economy becomes increasingly interconnected, the actions of one central bank can have spillover effects on other countries. This has led to calls for greater transparency and communication among central banks to minimize the potential negative impacts of their policies on the global financial system.

In conclusion, the Federal Reserve's role in the global financial system is significant and multifaceted. Its monetary policy decisions, coordination efforts with other central banks, and actions during times of crisis all have implications that extend beyond U.S. borders. While the Federal Reserve's actions aim to promote stability and economic growth, they can also have unintended consequences and generate debates about the appropriate role of central banks in the global economy. Understanding the Federal Reserve's role in the global financial system is crucial for comprehending the complexities of the modern interconnected world.

7.2 International Monetary Policy and the Federal Reserve

The Federal Reserve, as the central bank of the United States, plays a significant role not only in the domestic economy but also in the global financial system. Its policies and actions have far-reaching implications for international monetary policy and the stability of global markets. In this section, we will explore the relationship between the Federal Reserve and the international monetary system, the impacts of its policies on global markets, and the challenges it faces in maintaining stability in an interconnected world.

The Federal Reserve's Role in the Global Financial System

The Federal Reserve's actions and policies have a profound impact on the global financial system. As the issuer of the world's primary reserve currency, the U.S. dollar, the Federal Reserve's decisions can influence global interest rates, exchange rates, and capital flows. The U.S. dollar's status as the dominant international currency means that changes in U.S. monetary policy can have spillover effects on other countries and their economies.

One of the key ways in which the Federal Reserve affects the global financial system is through its control over interest rates. By adjusting the federal funds rate, which is the rate at which banks lend to each other overnight, the Federal Reserve can influence borrowing costs not only in the United States but also in other countries. Changes in U.S. interest rates can attract or repel foreign investors, impacting capital flows and exchange rates.

Furthermore, the Federal Reserve's monetary policy decisions can have implications for global financial stability. For example, during times of economic crisis, such as the global financial crisis of 2008, the Federal Reserve has taken extraordinary measures to provide liquidity to financial markets not only in the United States but also globally. These actions, such as the implementation of swap lines with foreign central banks, helped stabilize global financial markets and prevent a further escalation of the crisis.

Impacts of Federal Reserve Actions on Global Markets

The Federal Reserve's policies and actions can have both positive and negative impacts on global markets. On the positive side, the Federal Reserve's efforts to stabilize the U.S. economy and maintain price stability can contribute to global economic growth and stability. By implementing sound monetary policies, the Federal Reserve can help promote confidence in the U.S. dollar and attract foreign investment.

However, the Federal Reserve's actions can also create challenges for other countries and their economies. For example, when the Federal Reserve tightens monetary policy by raising interest rates, it can lead to capital outflows from emerging markets as investors seek higher returns in the United States. This can put pressure on the currencies and financial systems of these countries, potentially leading to financial instability.

Another challenge arises from the potential spillover effects of unconventional monetary policies, such as quantitative easing (QE). When the Federal Reserve engages in QE, it purchases large quantities of government bonds and other securities, injecting liquidity into the financial system. While this can stimulate economic growth and support asset prices in the United States, it can also lead to excessive liquidity and asset price inflation in other countries, creating risks of financial imbalances.

The Federal Reserve's Role in International Cooperation

Given the interconnected nature of the global financial system, international cooperation is crucial for maintaining stability and addressing common challenges. The Federal Reserve actively participates in international forums and collaborates with other central banks and international organizations to promote coordination and cooperation.

For example, the Federal Reserve is a member of the International Monetary Fund (IMF) and the Bank for International Settlements (BIS), which serve as platforms for central banks to exchange information, discuss policy issues, and coordinate actions. Through these channels, the Federal Reserve contributes to the development of international monetary policy frameworks and the sharing of best practices.

However, international cooperation is not without its challenges. Divergent national interests, differing economic conditions, and varying policy priorities can make it difficult to reach consensus on key issues. Moreover, the Federal Reserve's actions are primarily driven by domestic considerations, as its mandate is to promote maximum employment and price stability in the United States. This can sometimes create tensions with other countries that may have different policy objectives.

In recent years, there have been calls for greater international policy coordination, particularly in the areas of monetary policy and exchange rate management. As the global economy becomes increasingly interconnected, the actions of one central bank can have significant implications for others. Enhancing cooperation and communication among central banks can help mitigate the risks of policy spillovers and promote global financial stability.

In conclusion, the Federal Reserve's role in the international monetary system is crucial. Its policies and actions have far-reaching implications for global markets, influencing interest rates, exchange rates, and capital flows. While the Federal Reserve's actions can contribute to global economic stability, they can also create challenges for other countries. International cooperation and coordination are essential for addressing these challenges and promoting global financial stability in an interconnected world.

7.3 Impacts of Federal Reserve Actions on Global Markets

The actions and decisions of the Federal Reserve, as the central bank of the United States, have far-reaching effects on global markets. The Federal Reserve's policies and interventions have the potential to influence not only the domestic economy but also the global financial system. In this section, we will explore the impacts of Federal Reserve actions on global markets and the consequences they can have on economies around the world.

One of the primary ways in which the Federal Reserve affects global markets is through its monetary policy decisions. The Federal Reserve has the power to adjust interest rates, control the money supply, and influence the availability of credit. These actions can have significant implications for global financial markets, as they impact the cost of borrowing and the overall liquidity of the global economy.

When the Federal Reserve raises interest rates, it becomes more expensive for businesses and individuals to borrow money. This can lead to a decrease in investment and consumer spending, both domestically and internationally. As a result, global markets may experience a slowdown in economic activity, as businesses and consumers become more cautious with their spending.

Conversely, when the Federal Reserve lowers interest rates, it becomes cheaper to borrow money, which can stimulate economic growth and increase investment. This can have positive effects on global markets, as increased economic activity in the United States can create opportunities for businesses and investors around the world.

Another way in which the Federal Reserve's actions impact global markets is through its management of the U.S. dollar. As the world's reserve currency, the U.S. dollar plays a crucial role in international trade and finance. The Federal Reserve's monetary policy decisions can influence the value of the

U.S. dollar, which in turn affects exchange rates and trade flows between countries.

For example, if the Federal Reserve pursues a policy of monetary easing, such as quantitative easing, it can lead to a depreciation of the U.S. dollar. A weaker dollar can make U.S. exports more competitive, as they become relatively cheaper for foreign buyers. This can boost U.S. exports and potentially improve the trade balance. However, it can also have negative consequences for other countries whose currencies appreciate against the dollar, making their exports relatively more expensive.

On the other hand, if the Federal Reserve tightens monetary policy and raises interest rates, it can strengthen the U.S. dollar. A stronger dollar can make U.S. exports more expensive, potentially leading to a decrease in demand for U.S. goods and services. This can have a negative impact on global markets, particularly for countries that rely heavily on exports to the United States.

The Federal Reserve's actions also have implications for global financial stability. The central bank's response to financial crises and its role as a lender of last resort can help mitigate the impact of crises on global markets. For example, during the 2008 financial crisis, the Federal Reserve implemented various measures to stabilize the financial system, including providing liquidity to banks and purchasing troubled assets. These actions helped prevent a complete collapse of the global financial system and contributed to the recovery of global markets.

However, the Federal Reserve's actions can also create challenges for global markets. For instance, the unconventional monetary policies pursued by the Federal Reserve, such as quantitative easing, have raised concerns about potential spillover effects on other countries. These policies can lead to capital flows into emerging markets, which can create volatility and instability in their financial markets.

Furthermore, the Federal Reserve's decisions can have unintended consequences for global markets. For example, when the Federal Reserve began to taper its quantitative easing program in 2013, it led to a sharp increase in U.S. Treasury yields. This had a ripple effect on global bond markets, causing yields to rise in other countries as well. This episode highlighted the interconnectedness of global financial markets and the potential for Federal Reserve actions to have widespread effects.

In conclusion, the actions and decisions of the Federal Reserve have significant impacts on global markets. Through its monetary policy decisions, management of the U.S. dollar, and role in maintaining financial stability, the Federal Reserve can influence economic activity, exchange rates, and financial market conditions around the world. However, these actions can also create challenges and unintended consequences for global markets, underscoring the importance of understanding the role of the Federal Reserve in the global economy.

Critiques and Controversies Surrounding the Federal Reserve

8.1 Arguments Against the Federal Reserve

The Federal Reserve, as a central banking system in the United States, has been a subject of criticism and controversy since its establishment in 1913. While it was created with the intention of stabilizing the economy and ensuring financial security, there are several arguments against the Federal Reserve that have been put forth by various individuals and groups. These arguments range from concerns about its power and influence to allegations of conspiracy and corruption. In this section, we will explore some of the main arguments against the Federal Reserve.

Lack of Accountability and Transparency

One of the primary arguments against the Federal Reserve is the perceived lack of accountability and transparency. Critics argue that the Federal Reserve operates with a significant degree of independence from the government, which raises concerns about democratic oversight and public accountability. Unlike other government agencies, the Federal Reserve is not subject to regular audits by the Government Accountability Office (GAO), leading to questions about the extent of its financial activities and decision-making processes.

Concentration of Power

Another argument against the Federal Reserve is the concentration of power it holds. Critics contend that the Federal Reserve, as a central bank, wields immense influence over the economy and financial system, which can potentially lead to abuses of power. They argue that the Federal Reserve's ability to control interest rates, regulate banks, and conduct monetary policy gives it an undue level of authority that can be easily manipulated by those in charge.

Economic Manipulation and Financial Crises

Critics of the Federal Reserve also argue that its policies and actions have contributed to economic manipulation and financial crises. They claim that the Federal Reserve's control over interest rates and money supply allows it to artificially stimulate or suppress economic activity, leading to booms and busts in the economy. Some argue that the Federal Reserve's response to the 2008 financial crisis, such as the implementation of quantitative easing, only served to exacerbate the problem and benefit the financial elite at the expense of the general public.

Inflation and Devaluation of Currency

Another concern raised by critics is the potential for inflation and devaluation of the currency. They argue that the Federal Reserve's ability to create money out of thin air, through the process of fractional reserve banking and open market operations, can lead to an increase in the money supply and subsequent inflation. Critics contend that this inflation erodes the purchasing power of the currency, disproportionately affecting the middle and lower classes.

Allegations of Conspiracy and Corruption

Perhaps the most controversial arguments against the Federal Reserve are the allegations of conspiracy and corruption. Some critics claim that the Federal Reserve is controlled by a secretive group of international bankers who manipulate the economy and financial markets for their own benefit. These conspiracy theories often involve claims of hidden agendas, such as the desire to establish a global currency or exert control over governments and economies worldwide. It is important to note that these allegations lack substantial evidence and are widely dismissed by mainstream economists and experts.

Impact on Small Businesses and Savers

Critics also argue that the Federal Reserve's policies disproportionately favor large financial institutions and Wall Street at the expense of small businesses and savers. They contend that the low-interest-rate environment created by the Federal Reserve benefits big banks and encourages risky behavior, while making it difficult for small businesses to access affordable credit. Additionally, savers who rely on interest income from their savings accounts are negatively impacted by the low-interest-rate policies of the Federal Reserve.

In conclusion, there are several arguments against the Federal Reserve that have been put forth by critics. These arguments range from concerns about accountability and transparency to allegations of conspiracy and corruption. Critics argue that the concentration of power, economic manipulation, inflation, and the impact on small businesses and savers are all reasons to question the role and effectiveness of the Federal Reserve. While it is important to critically examine and debate the functions and policies of the Federal Reserve, it is equally important to separate legitimate concerns from unfounded conspiracy theories.

8.2 Conspiracy Theories and the Federal Reserve

The Federal Reserve has long been a subject of controversy and conspiracy theories. These theories often stem from a lack of understanding or misinformation about the central banking system and its operations. While it is important to critically examine institutions and question their actions, it is equally important to separate fact from fiction when discussing the Federal Reserve.

One of the most prevalent conspiracy theories surrounding the Federal Reserve is the notion that it is a secretive and shadowy organization controlled by a small group of powerful individuals. This theory suggests that the Federal Reserve operates outside of the control of the government and serves the interests of a select few. However, this claim is not supported by the facts.

The Federal Reserve is a government-created institution, established by an act of Congress in 1913. It operates under the oversight of the U.S. government and is subject to congressional audits and scrutiny. The Federal Reserve's decision-making process involves a complex system of checks and balances, with input from various stakeholders, including the Board of Governors, regional Federal Reserve Banks, and the Federal Open Market Committee.

Another conspiracy theory suggests that the Federal Reserve intentionally manipulates the economy for the benefit of a small elite. This theory often revolves around the idea that the Federal Reserve deliberately causes economic crises, such as recessions or depressions, to consolidate power and wealth. However, there is no credible evidence to support these claims.

The Federal Reserve's primary mandate is to promote price stability, maximum employment, and moderate long-term interest rates. Its actions are guided by economic data, analysis, and the expertise of its policymakers. While the Federal Reserve's decisions can have significant impacts on the economy, they are made with the intention of maintaining a stable and healthy financial system.

It is important to note that conspiracy theories surrounding the Federal Reserve often overlook the complexities of the global financial system. Economic events and crises are the result of a multitude of factors, including global market forces, fiscal policies, and the actions of various financial institutions. Blaming the Federal Reserve alone for economic downturns oversimplifies the complex nature of the global economy.

Presidential opposition to the Federal Reserve has also fueled conspiracy theories. One of the most notable examples is President John F. Kennedy's alleged attempt to end the Federal Reserve. Some conspiracy theorists claim that Kennedy's executive order 11110, which authorized the issuance of silver certificates, was an attempt to undermine the Federal Reserve's control over the money supply. However, this claim is unfounded.

Executive order 11110 was primarily aimed at increasing the circulation of silver certificates and had little impact on the Federal Reserve's operations. Kennedy's administration recognized the importance of the Federal Reserve in maintaining a stable financial system and did not seek to dismantle it. Unfortunately, Kennedy's presidency was cut short by his assassination, leaving room for speculation and conspiracy theories to emerge.

Other presidents, such as Richard Nixon and Ronald Reagan, have also faced accusations of opposing the Federal Reserve. Nixon's decision to temporarily suspend the convertibility of the U.S. dollar into gold in 1971 and Reagan's criticism of the Federal Reserve's monetary policies have been cited as evidence of their opposition. However, these actions were driven by economic considerations and were not attempts to dismantle the Federal Reserve.

In conclusion, conspiracy theories surrounding the Federal Reserve often stem from a lack of understanding or misinformation about its operations and purpose. The Federal Reserve is a government-created institution that operates under the oversight of the U.S. government. While it is important to critically examine institutions and question their actions, it is equally important to base these examinations on factual information. The Federal Reserve's primary mandate is to promote price stability, maximum employment, and moderate long-term interest rates. Blaming the Federal Reserve alone for economic crises oversimplifies the complex nature of the global financial system.

8.3 Controversial Decisions and Policies

Throughout its history, the Federal Reserve has made several controversial decisions and implemented policies that have sparked debates and criticism. These decisions and policies have had far-reaching implications for the economy, the banking system, and the American people. In this section, we will explore some of the most contentious actions taken by the Federal Reserve and the controversies surrounding them.

The Great Depression and the Federal Reserve's Response

One of the most significant controversies surrounding the Federal Reserve is its role in the Great Depression of the 1930s. Many economists and historians argue that the Federal Reserve's monetary policies exacerbated the severity and duration of the economic downturn. The central bank's decision to tighten monetary policy by raising interest rates and reducing the money supply is believed to have contributed to the contraction of credit and the subsequent collapse of banks.

Critics argue that the Federal Reserve's failure to act as a lender of last resort during the banking crisis worsened the situation. By not providing sufficient liquidity to the banking system, the Federal Reserve allowed numerous banks to fail, leading to a wave of bank runs and further economic instability.

Quantitative Easing and Unconventional Monetary Policies

In response to the 2008 financial crisis, the Federal Reserve implemented a series of unconventional monetary policies, including quantitative easing (QE). QE involved the purchase of large quantities of government bonds and other securities to inject liquidity into the financial system and stimulate economic growth.

While these policies were aimed at stabilizing the economy and preventing a deeper recession, they have been subject to intense debate and criticism. Critics argue that QE has artificially inflated asset prices, leading to potential bubbles in the stock and housing markets. They also express concerns about the long-term consequences of the massive expansion of the Federal Reserve's balance sheet and the potential for future inflation.

Bailouts and Too Big to Fail

Another controversial decision made by the Federal Reserve was its involvement in the bailouts of large financial institutions during the 2008 crisis. The central bank provided emergency loans and assistance to prevent the collapse of major banks and other financial firms deemed "too big to fail."

Critics argue that these bailouts created a moral hazard by rewarding risky behavior and encouraging future financial recklessness. They contend that the Federal Reserve's actions protected the interests of Wall Street at the expense of Main Street, as ordinary taxpayers were left to bear the burden of the crisis while the financial industry was rescued.

Interest Rate Manipulation and Market Distortions

The Federal Reserve's control over interest rates has also been a subject of controversy. Critics argue that the central bank's manipulation of interest rates through its monetary policy decisions distorts market signals and interferes with the natural functioning of the economy.

Low-interest rates, maintained for an extended period, can encourage excessive borrowing and risk-taking, potentially leading to asset bubbles and financial instability. On the other hand, high-interest rates can hinder economic growth and make it more difficult for businesses and individuals to access credit.

Lack of Transparency and Accountability

One recurring criticism of the Federal Reserve is its perceived lack of transparency and accountability. Critics argue that the central bank operates with a high degree of secrecy, making it difficult for the public to fully understand its decision-making processes and the factors influencing its policies.

Calls for increased transparency and accountability have led to debates about the need for greater congressional oversight and audits of the Federal Reserve. Advocates argue that a more transparent central bank would enhance public trust and allow for a more informed discussion about its actions and policies.

In conclusion, the Federal Reserve has faced significant controversy throughout its history due to its decisions and policies. From its role in the Great Depression to its response to the 2008 financial crisis, the central bank's actions have been subject to intense scrutiny and criticism. The debates surrounding the Federal Reserve's decisions highlight the complex nature of monetary policy and the challenges of balancing economic stability, market dynamics, and public accountability.

Proposals for Reforming the Federal Reserve

9.1 Calls for Structural Changes

Since its establishment in 1913, the Federal Reserve has been a subject of intense scrutiny and criticism. Over the years, various individuals and groups have called for structural changes to the Federal Reserve system in an attempt to address perceived flaws and improve its functionality. These calls for reform have come from both within and outside the government, and have focused on a range of issues including transparency, accountability, and the concentration of power within the institution.

One of the primary concerns raised by critics of the Federal Reserve is the concentration of power in the hands of a few individuals. The Federal Reserve is governed by a Board of Governors, which consists of seven members appointed by the President and confirmed by the Senate. Critics argue that this concentration of power undermines the democratic principles upon which the United States was founded. They argue that the Federal Reserve should be more representative of the American people and that its decision-making process should be more transparent.

Calls for structural changes to the Federal Reserve often center around the composition of the Board of Governors. Critics argue that the Board should include a broader range of voices and perspectives, including representatives from different regions of the country and different sectors of the economy. They argue that this would help to ensure that the interests of all Americans are taken into account in the decision-making process.

Another area of concern is the relationship between the Federal Reserve and the banking industry. Critics argue that the Federal Reserve is too closely aligned with the interests of the banking industry and that this creates a conflict of interest. They argue that the Federal Reserve should be more independent and should prioritize the interests of the American people over the interests of the banking industry.

One proposal for reforming the Federal Reserve is to increase the transparency and accountability of the institution. Critics argue that the Federal Reserve operates with too much secrecy and that this undermines public trust in the institution. They argue that the Federal Reserve should be subject to greater oversight and that its decision-making process should be more transparent. This could include regular audits of the Federal Reserve's activities and increased disclosure of its decision-making processes.

Another proposal is to decentralize the power of the Federal Reserve. Critics argue that the concentration of power in the hands of a few individuals undermines the democratic principles upon which the United States was founded. They argue that power should be more evenly distributed among the various regional Federal Reserve banks and that decision-making should be more collaborative.

Some critics have called for the Federal Reserve to be abolished altogether and replaced with a different monetary system. They argue that the Federal Reserve's control over the money supply and interest rates gives it too much power and that this power should be decentralized. They propose alternative monetary systems, such as a return to the gold standard or the adoption of a cryptocurrency-based system.

It is important to note that proposals for reforming the Federal Reserve are not without controversy. There are differing opinions on the best way to address the perceived flaws in the system, and there is often significant debate and disagreement among policymakers and economists. Additionally, any proposed changes to the Federal Reserve would require careful consideration and analysis to ensure that they do not have unintended consequences or disrupt the stability of the financial system.

In conclusion, calls for structural changes to the Federal Reserve have been a recurring theme throughout its history. Critics argue that the concentration of power, lack of transparency, and close alignment with the banking industry undermine the institution's effectiveness and democratic principles. Proposals for reform range from increasing transparency and accountability to decentralizing power and even abolishing the Federal Reserve altogether. However, any proposed changes must be carefully considered to ensure that they do not have unintended consequences or disrupt the stability of the financial system.

9.2 Alternative Monetary Systems

As we delve deeper into the discussion surrounding the Federal Reserve, it becomes increasingly important to explore alternative monetary systems that have been proposed as potential alternatives to the current central banking model. While the Federal Reserve has been the dominant force in the United States' monetary policy for over a century, there have been various alternative systems suggested by economists, scholars, and policymakers. In this section, we will examine some of these alternative monetary systems and evaluate their potential merits and drawbacks.

The Gold Standard

One of the most well-known alternative monetary systems is the gold standard. Under the gold standard, a country's currency is directly linked to a fixed amount of gold. Proponents of the gold standard argue that it provides stability and limits the ability of central banks to manipulate the money supply. They believe that tying the value of money to a tangible asset like gold prevents inflation and promotes fiscal discipline.

However, critics of the gold standard argue that it can be inflexible and restrict the ability of governments to respond to economic crises. They contend that the supply of gold is limited, and as economies grow, the money supply may not be able to keep pace, leading to deflationary pressures. Additionally, the gold standard does not account for the complexities of modern economies, such as the need for monetary policy to address unemployment and promote economic growth.

Free Banking

Another alternative monetary system that has been proposed is the concept of free banking. Free banking advocates argue for the removal of government control over the issuance of currency and the establishment of a competitive banking system. Under this system, banks would be free to issue their own currencies, and the market would determine which currencies are accepted and valued.

Proponents of free banking argue that it promotes competition, innovation, and efficiency in the banking sector. They believe that without government interference, banks would be incentivized to maintain the value of their currencies and ensure the stability of the financial system. Additionally, they argue that free banking would eliminate the need for a central bank and reduce the risk of government manipulation of the money supply.

Critics of free banking, however, raise concerns about the potential for instability and uncertainty in the monetary system. They argue that without a central authority to regulate and oversee the banking sector, there is a higher risk of bank failures and financial crises. Additionally, they contend that the lack of a unified currency could create transactional difficulties and hinder economic integration.

Digital Currencies

In recent years, the rise of digital currencies, such as Bitcoin and other cryptocurrencies, has sparked discussions about the potential for alternative monetary systems. These digital currencies operate on decentralized networks and utilize cryptographic technology to secure transactions and control the creation of new units.

Proponents of digital currencies argue that they offer increased transparency, security, and efficiency compared to traditional fiat currencies. They believe that the decentralized nature of digital currencies reduces the risk of government manipulation and provides individuals with greater control over their financial transactions. Additionally, they argue that digital currencies have the potential to promote financial inclusion by providing access to banking services for the unbanked population.

However, critics of digital currencies raise concerns about their volatility, lack of regulation, and potential for facilitating illicit activities. They argue that the absence of a central authority to oversee and regulate digital currencies poses risks to financial stability and consumer protection. Additionally, they contend that the energy-intensive nature of cryptocurrency mining has negative environmental implications.

Local Currencies and Complementary Currencies

Another alternative monetary system that has gained attention in recent years is the use of local currencies or complementary currencies. These currencies are typically used within specific communities or regions and are designed to promote local economic activity and strengthen community ties.

Proponents of local currencies argue that they encourage local spending, support small businesses, and foster community resilience. They believe that by circulating within a specific geographic area, local currencies can help to retain wealth within the community and reduce dependence on external economic forces. Additionally, they argue that local currencies can promote social and environmental goals by incentivizing sustainable practices and supporting local initiatives.

Critics of local currencies raise concerns about their limited acceptance and potential for creating economic fragmentation. They argue that the use of multiple currencies within a single economy can create transactional difficulties and hinder economic efficiency. Additionally, they contend that local currencies may not be able to provide the same level of stability and liquidity as national currencies.

In conclusion, while the Federal Reserve has been the dominant force in the United States' monetary system for over a century, alternative monetary systems have been proposed as potential alternatives. These include the gold standard, free banking, digital currencies, and local currencies. Each of these systems has its own merits and drawbacks, and the choice of an alternative monetary system would require careful consideration of various economic, social, and political factors. As we move forward, it is essential to continue exploring and evaluating these alternatives to ensure a robust and resilient monetary system that serves the best interests of the American people.

9.3 The Future of the Federal Reserve

As we delve into the future of the Federal Reserve, it is essential to understand the historical context and the impact it has had on the American people. The Federal Reserve, established in 1913, has been a subject of controversy and debate since its inception. While it was created with the intention of stabilizing the economy and providing a central banking system, its influence and power have evolved over time.

The Need for Reform

Critics argue that the Federal Reserve has become too powerful and lacks the necessary transparency and accountability. Calls for reform have been growing louder in recent years, with many advocating for structural changes to the system. The future of the Federal Reserve will likely be shaped by these reform proposals and the public's demand for a more accountable and transparent central banking system.

Calls for Structural Changes

One of the primary proposals for reforming the Federal Reserve is to increase its transparency and accountability. Critics argue that the lack of transparency has allowed the Federal Reserve to operate without proper oversight, leading to potential abuses of power. Advocates for reform suggest implementing measures such as regular audits of the Federal Reserve's activities to ensure transparency and accountability.

Additionally, there have been calls to change the structure of the Federal Reserve itself. Some propose reducing the influence of private banks on the Federal Reserve's decision-making process. They argue that the current system, where private banks have representation on the Federal Reserve's Board of Governors, creates a potential conflict of interest. Instead, they suggest a more independent and publicly accountable central banking system.

Alternative Monetary Systems

In addition to calls for structural changes, there have been discussions about alternative monetary systems that could replace or supplement the Federal Reserve. One such proposal is the adoption of a gold standard, where the value of the currency is tied to a fixed amount of gold. Advocates argue that this would provide stability and prevent inflationary practices by the central bank.

Another alternative monetary system that has gained attention is the use of cryptocurrencies or blockchain technology. Proponents argue that decentralized digital currencies could provide a more transparent and secure financial system, reducing the need for a central bank like the Federal Reserve.

The Role of Technology

The future of the Federal Reserve is also likely to be influenced by advancements in technology. The rise of digital currencies and financial technologies has the potential to reshape the banking industry and the role of central banks. As technology continues to evolve, the Federal Reserve may need to adapt its policies and regulations to keep pace with the changing financial landscape.

Balancing Stability and Flexibility

One of the challenges the Federal Reserve faces is striking the right balance between maintaining economic stability and allowing for flexibility in response to changing economic conditions. The Federal Reserve's primary mandate is to promote maximum employment, stable prices, and moderate long-term interest rates. However, the methods and tools used to achieve these goals have been a subject of debate.

The future of the Federal Reserve will likely involve ongoing discussions about the appropriate monetary policy framework. Some argue for a more rules-based approach, where the Federal Reserve follows a predetermined set of guidelines, reducing the potential for discretionary decision-making. Others advocate for a more flexible approach, allowing the Federal Reserve to respond to unforeseen economic circumstances.

Public Perception and Awareness

Another crucial aspect of the future of the Federal Reserve is the public's perception and awareness of its role and functions. Many Americans have limited knowledge and understanding of the Federal Reserve and its impact on the economy. Increasing public education and awareness about the Federal Reserve's role could lead to a more informed and engaged citizenry, shaping the future of the institution.

The Role of the American People

Ultimately, the future of the Federal Reserve will be influenced by the American people and their demands for a more accountable and transparent central banking system. As public awareness and understanding of the Federal Reserve grow, so too will the pressure for reform. The American people have the power to shape the future of the Federal Reserve through their engagement with policymakers and their demand for a more equitable and effective monetary system.

In conclusion, the future of the Federal Reserve is uncertain, but calls for reform and increased transparency are likely to shape its trajectory. Structural changes, alternative monetary systems, advancements in technology, and public awareness will all play a role in determining the future of this influential institution. As the American people continue to engage in discussions about the Federal Reserve, it is crucial to understand its history, impact, and potential for change.

The Federal Reserve and the American People

10.1 Public Perception and Awareness

Public perception and awareness of the Federal Reserve have played a significant role in shaping the ongoing debate surrounding its existence and operations. The Federal Reserve, as the central banking system of the United States, has often been a subject of controversy and scrutiny. Understanding the public's perception and level of awareness is crucial in comprehending the broader implications of the Federal Reserve's actions and the potential for reform.

The public's perception of the Federal Reserve has been influenced by various factors, including historical events, economic conditions, and political discourse. Over the years, the Federal Reserve has been both praised and criticized, leading to a diverse range of opinions among the American people.

One of the key aspects of public perception is the level of awareness regarding the Federal Reserve's role and functions. Unfortunately, studies have shown that a significant portion of the American population lacks a clear understanding of the Federal Reserve and its operations. This lack of awareness can be attributed to several factors, including the complexity of the subject matter and the limited emphasis on financial education in the general curriculum.

To fully grasp the public's perception and awareness, it is essential to examine the historical context surrounding the creation of the Federal Reserve. Prior to its establishment in 1913, the American people had limited direct control over the government's monetary policy. The absence of a central banking system meant that decisions regarding the nation's currency, interest rates, and financial stability were largely in the hands of private banks and the government.

The creation of the Federal Reserve aimed to address the need for a more stable and centralized banking system. However, this shift in power dynamics resulted in a loss of direct control for the American people. The Federal Reserve Act granted the newly formed institution significant authority over monetary policy, including the ability to set interest rates and regulate the money supply. As a result, the American people's influence over these crucial economic decisions was significantly diminished.

While the Federal Reserve Act was met with some opposition at the time of its passage, it was not until the presidency of John F. Kennedy that a notable attempt to challenge the Federal Reserve emerged. President Kennedy, recognizing the potential influence of the Federal Reserve on the economy, sought to curtail its power. He aimed to transfer the authority to issue currency from the Federal Reserve to the U.S. Treasury, effectively reducing the central bank's control over the money supply.

Unfortunately, President Kennedy's efforts to challenge the Federal Reserve were cut short by his assassination in 1963. Subsequent presidents, including Richard Nixon and Ronald Reagan, expressed concerns about the Federal Reserve's influence but did not actively pursue its abolition or significant reform. The opposition to the Federal Reserve from various presidents has often been met with limited success, as the institution's power and influence have remained largely intact.

The public's perception of the Federal Reserve and its awareness of its operations have been shaped by these historical events and the subsequent political discourse. However, it is important to note that public opinion on the Federal Reserve is not monolithic. There are individuals and groups who strongly support the institution and believe in its ability to maintain economic stability. Conversely, there are those who question its legitimacy and advocate for its reform or abolition.

In recent years, there has been a growing movement calling for increased transparency and accountability of the Federal Reserve. Critics argue that the lack of transparency surrounding the institution's decision-making processes and the limited oversight contribute to public distrust and misunderstanding. Efforts to audit the Federal Reserve and increase public access to its operations have gained traction, reflecting a desire for greater public awareness and involvement.

In conclusion, public perception and awareness of the Federal Reserve are crucial factors in understanding the ongoing debate surrounding its existence and operations. The creation of the Federal Reserve resulted in a shift in power dynamics, diminishing the American people's direct control over monetary policy. While there have been attempts by presidents, including JFK, to challenge the Federal Reserve, the institution's power has remained largely intact. The public's perception of the Federal Reserve is diverse, with varying levels of awareness and opinions. Efforts to increase transparency and accountability reflect a growing desire for greater public involvement and understanding of the Federal Reserve's role in the economy.

10.2 Education and Understanding

Education and understanding are crucial when it comes to unraveling the truth behind the Federal Reserve. The complex nature of the Federal Reserve's operations and its impact on the economy necessitate a well-informed public. In this section, we will explore the importance of education and understanding in relation to the Federal Reserve and its role in shaping the American economy.

The Need for Education

To fully comprehend the Federal Reserve and its implications, it is essential to have a solid foundation of knowledge. Unfortunately, the average American's understanding of the Federal Reserve is often limited or distorted. This lack of education can lead to misconceptions and conspiracy theories, hindering meaningful discussions about the institution's merits and flaws.

Education plays a vital role in dispelling myths and promoting informed discussions. By providing accurate and accessible information about the Federal Reserve, individuals can develop a more nuanced understanding of its purpose, functions, and impact on the economy. This knowledge empowers citizens to engage in constructive debates and make informed decisions regarding the Federal Reserve's future.

The Role of Schools and Universities

One avenue for promoting education and understanding about the Federal Reserve is through the education system. Schools and universities can play a crucial role in teaching students about the Federal Reserve's history, structure, and functions. By incorporating this topic into the curriculum, students can develop a foundational understanding of the institution and its significance.

Educators can utilize various teaching methods, such as lectures, discussions, and case studies, to engage students in critical thinking and analysis. By examining historical events and economic theories related to the Federal

Reserve, students can gain a deeper understanding of its impact on the American economy and society as a whole.

Public Awareness Campaigns

In addition to formal education, public awareness campaigns can help bridge the knowledge gap surrounding the Federal Reserve. These campaigns can utilize various mediums, such as television, radio, social media, and public forums, to disseminate accurate information and promote understanding.

Public awareness campaigns can focus on debunking common misconceptions and conspiracy theories surrounding the Federal Reserve. By presenting facts and evidence, these campaigns can help individuals distinguish between legitimate concerns and baseless claims. Moreover, they can encourage citizens to engage in constructive dialogue and hold informed discussions about the Federal Reserve's policies and practices.

Independent Research and Analysis

Individuals can also take the initiative to educate themselves about the Federal Reserve through independent research and analysis. By seeking out reputable sources, such as books, scholarly articles, and reputable news outlets, individuals can gain a comprehensive understanding of the institution.

Independent research allows individuals to critically evaluate different perspectives and form their own opinions about the Federal Reserve. It enables them to delve into the historical context, examine economic theories, and analyze the institution's impact on the American economy. By engaging in this process, individuals can contribute to informed discussions and advocate for necessary reforms or changes.

The Importance of Understanding

Education and understanding are crucial for holding the Federal Reserve accountable and ensuring its policies align with the best interests of the

American people. Without a well-informed citizenry, it becomes challenging to assess the Federal Reserve's performance and advocate for necessary reforms.

Understanding the Federal Reserve's history, functions, and impact empowers individuals to engage in meaningful discussions and contribute to the ongoing dialogue surrounding the institution. It allows citizens to evaluate the Federal Reserve's policies critically and voice their concerns or support based on informed analysis.

Moving Forward

In an increasingly complex and interconnected world, education and understanding are essential for navigating the intricacies of the Federal Reserve. By promoting education through schools, universities, public awareness campaigns, and independent research, individuals can develop a comprehensive understanding of the institution's role in shaping the American economy.

As the American people become more educated and informed about the Federal Reserve, they can actively participate in discussions about its policies and practices. This engagement fosters a more transparent and accountable Federal Reserve, ensuring that its decisions align with the best interests of the American people.

In the next section, we will explore the role of the American people in relation to the Federal Reserve and how their involvement can shape the institution's future.

10.3 The Role of the American People

The establishment of the Federal Reserve brought about significant changes in the power dynamics between the American people and the government. Before delving into the specific powers that the American people had over the government before the creation of the Federal Reserve, it is important to understand the need for a central bank and the circumstances that led to its formation.

The Need for a Central Bank

In the early years of the United States, the country faced numerous challenges related to its financial system. The absence of a central bank meant that there was no unified authority to regulate and stabilize the economy. The lack of a central bank led to frequent financial panics, economic instability, and a lack of confidence in the banking system.

The proponents of a central bank argued that it would provide stability, promote economic growth, and prevent financial crises. They believed that a central bank could effectively manage the money supply, regulate interest rates, and act as a lender of last resort during times of financial distress.

The Power Dynamics Before the Federal Reserve

Before the establishment of the Federal Reserve, the American people had certain powers over the government that played a crucial role in shaping policies and decision-making. One of the significant powers was the ability to exercise veto power through their elected representatives. The American people had the power to elect officials who could veto legislation that they deemed unfavorable or against their interests.

This power allowed the American people to have a direct influence on the government's actions and policies. It provided a system of checks and balances, ensuring that the government remained accountable to the people it served.

The Creation of the Federal Reserve and the Loss of Power

The creation of the Federal Reserve in 1913 brought about a shift in the power dynamics between the American people and the government. With the establishment of the central bank, the power to control the nation's monetary policy and regulate the banking system was transferred to a small group of unelected officials.

The Federal Reserve Act granted the central bank significant autonomy and independence from political interference. This meant that the American people had limited control over the decisions made by the Federal Reserve, as its policies were determined by a board of governors appointed by the President and confirmed by the Senate.

The loss of power was further exacerbated by the complexity of the Federal Reserve's operations. The intricacies of monetary policy and banking regulations made it challenging for the average American citizen to fully comprehend and participate in the decision-making process.

Presidential Opposition to the Federal Reserve

John F. Kennedy (JFK) was one of the notable presidents who expressed opposition to the Federal Reserve. He believed that the central bank's power and lack of transparency posed a threat to the democratic principles of the United States. JFK sought to limit the Federal Reserve's authority and return control of the monetary system to the government.

However, JFK's efforts to challenge the Federal Reserve were cut short by his assassination in 1963. Despite his opposition, the Federal Reserve continued to operate with its established powers and independence.

Other presidents, such as Andrew Jackson and Woodrow Wilson, also expressed concerns about the concentration of power in the hands of the central bank. However, their attempts to dismantle or significantly alter the Federal Reserve were largely unsuccessful.

Outcomes of Presidential Opposition

The opposition of presidents to the Federal Reserve has had limited success in altering the central bank's structure or powers. The Federal Reserve has remained a key institution in the American financial system, with its policies and decisions largely unaffected by presidential opposition.

However, the opposition of presidents and public figures has contributed to a broader public discourse on the role and influence of the Federal Reserve. It has sparked debates about the need for transparency, accountability, and potential reforms within the central bank.

While presidential opposition has not resulted in significant changes to the Federal Reserve's structure, it has played a role in raising awareness and fostering discussions about the central bank's impact on the economy and the American people.

In the next chapter, we will explore the influence of the Federal Reserve on the economy, including its monetary policy, impact on inflation and deflation, and its role in economic crises. Understanding these aspects is crucial in comprehending the broader implications of the Federal Reserve's actions and policies.

The Federal Reserve and the Political Landscape

11.1 Political Influence and Lobbying

The creation of the Federal Reserve brought about significant changes in the power dynamics between the American people and the government. Before the establishment of the Federal Reserve, the American people had certain powers, including the ability to influence government decisions through their elected representatives and the power of veto. However, with the advent of the Federal Reserve, some of these powers were diminished, leading to a shift in the balance of power.

One of the key powers that the American people had before the Federal Reserve was the power of veto. This power allowed the people to reject or block legislation that they deemed unfavorable or against their interests. The veto power was a crucial tool in ensuring that the government remained accountable to the people and that their voices were heard. However, with the establishment of the Federal Reserve, this power was significantly weakened. The Federal Reserve, as an independent entity, was granted the authority to make monetary policy decisions without direct oversight from the people or their elected representatives. This meant that the American people lost their ability to veto decisions made by the Federal Reserve, thereby reducing their influence over the government.

In addition to the loss of veto power, the American people also experienced a reduction in their overall influence over the government after the establishment of the Federal Reserve. The Federal Reserve, with its control over monetary policy, became a powerful institution that could directly impact the economy and financial system. This gave the Federal Reserve significant influence over government policies and decisions, often superseding the will of the people. As a result, the American people found themselves with limited avenues to challenge or influence the decisions made by the Federal Reserve, leading to a decrease in their overall power and influence.

John F. Kennedy (JFK) was one of the notable presidents who attempted to challenge the Federal Reserve. JFK recognized the potential dangers of a centralized banking system and sought to dismantle the Federal Reserve by returning the power to create money to the government. He issued Executive Order 11110, which authorized the Treasury Department to issue silver certificates, bypassing the Federal Reserve. However, JFK's efforts were short-lived, as he was assassinated shortly after issuing the order. The true motives behind his assassination remain a subject of debate and speculation.

Other presidents, such as Andrew Jackson and Abraham Lincoln, also expressed opposition to centralized banking systems and the power of private banks. Jackson, in particular, successfully dismantled the Second Bank of the United States, which was the precursor to the Federal Reserve. However, despite these oppositions, the Federal Reserve continued to exist and exert its influence over the American economy.

The outcome of presidential opposition to the Federal Reserve has varied throughout history. While some presidents, like Jackson, were successful in dismantling central banks, their efforts did not prevent the eventual establishment of the Federal Reserve. Other presidents, like JFK, faced significant challenges and were unable to fully challenge or dismantle the Federal Reserve before their terms ended. The power and influence of the Federal Reserve have proven to be resilient, often withstanding attempts to curtail or eliminate its authority.

In conclusion, the establishment of the Federal Reserve brought about a shift in the power dynamics between the American people and the government. The American people lost certain powers, such as the power of veto, and experienced a reduction in their overall influence over government decisions. Presidents like JFK and others have attempted to challenge the Federal Reserve, but their efforts have been met with varying degrees of success. The Federal Reserve's power and influence have remained intact, shaping the political landscape and impacting the lives of the American people.

11.2 Political Parties and the Federal Reserve

Political parties in the United States have played a significant role in shaping the country's economic policies and institutions. The Federal Reserve, as a central banking system, has not been immune to the influence of political parties. Throughout its history, the Federal Reserve has been subject to both support and opposition from various political parties, each with their own perspectives on monetary policy and the role of the central bank.

One of the key aspects to consider is the power dynamics before and after the establishment of the Federal Reserve. Prior to its creation, the American people had a certain level of power over the government, including the ability to influence economic policies through their elected representatives. The power of the people was reflected in the checks and balances system, which included the power of veto held by the President.

However, with the establishment of the Federal Reserve in 1913, the power dynamics began to shift. The central bank was given the authority to control the money supply, set interest rates, and regulate the banking system. This transfer of power from the people to the Federal Reserve meant that decisions regarding monetary policy were no longer directly influenced by the American people or their elected representatives. Instead, they were now in the hands of a group of unelected officials appointed by the President and confirmed by the Senate.

Over the years, several presidents have expressed opposition to the Federal Reserve and its policies. One notable example is President John F. Kennedy, who reportedly had concerns about the concentration of power in the hands of the central bank. Kennedy took steps to limit the influence of the Federal Reserve by issuing Executive Order 11110, which authorized the Treasury Department to issue silver certificates, bypassing the Federal Reserve's control over the money supply. However, Kennedy's efforts to challenge the Federal

Reserve were cut short by his assassination in 1963, leaving the long-term impact of his opposition uncertain.

Other presidents, such as Richard Nixon and Jimmy Carter, also expressed concerns about the Federal Reserve's policies. Nixon, in particular, blamed the central bank for contributing to inflation and sought to exert more control over its decision-making process. However, these attempts to challenge the Federal Reserve's authority were met with limited success, as the central bank maintained its independence and continued to operate with a certain degree of autonomy.

The outcomes of presidential opposition to the Federal Reserve have varied. While some presidents have been able to influence certain aspects of the central bank's policies, such as appointing individuals who align with their views to key positions, the overall structure and authority of the Federal Reserve have remained intact. The central bank's independence from political interference has been a cornerstone of its effectiveness in conducting monetary policy and maintaining financial stability.

It is important to note that the relationship between political parties and the Federal Reserve is complex and multifaceted. While some political parties have been more critical of the central bank and its policies, others have been more supportive. The Democratic and Republican parties, as the two major political parties in the United States, have both had members who have expressed varying degrees of support or opposition to the Federal Reserve.

In recent years, there has been a growing debate within political parties about the role and influence of the Federal Reserve. Some members of both parties have called for greater transparency and accountability, while others have advocated for more significant reforms, such as changes to the structure and governance of the central bank. These discussions reflect the ongoing tension between the desire for political control over monetary policy and the need for an independent central bank to maintain stability and promote economic growth.

In conclusion, political parties in the United States have had differing views on the Federal Reserve and its role in the economy. While some presidents, including JFK, have expressed opposition to the central bank, the overall structure and authority of the Federal Reserve have remained largely unchanged. The relationship between political parties and the Federal Reserve continues to evolve, with ongoing debates about transparency, accountability, and the appropriate balance between political control and central bank independence.

11.3 The Federal Reserve's Impact on Elections

The Federal Reserve, as a powerful institution, has had a significant impact on the political landscape of the United States, particularly in relation to elections. Its influence extends beyond the economic realm and has shaped the political discourse surrounding monetary policy and financial regulation. In this section, we will explore the ways in which the Federal Reserve's actions and policies have influenced elections and political dynamics.

One of the key aspects to consider is the Federal Reserve's ability to manipulate the economy through its control over monetary policy. The central bank has the power to influence interest rates, inflation, and overall economic stability. These factors play a crucial role in shaping the public's perception of the economy, which in turn can impact their voting behavior.

During election cycles, the Federal Reserve's decisions regarding interest rates and economic stimulus measures can have a direct impact on the overall state of the economy. For example, if the Federal Reserve decides to lower interest rates in the months leading up to an election, it can stimulate economic growth and potentially create a more favorable environment for the incumbent party. This can be seen as an attempt to boost the chances of the sitting president or party in power.

Conversely, the Federal Reserve can also tighten monetary policy by raising interest rates, which can have a dampening effect on economic growth. This can be a deliberate strategy to curb inflation or address other economic concerns. However, such actions can also have unintended consequences for the political landscape. If the economy experiences a downturn or recession due to the Federal Reserve's policies, it can create a challenging environment for the incumbent party, potentially leading to voter dissatisfaction and a desire for change.

Presidents and political candidates are often keenly aware of the Federal Reserve's influence on the economy and its potential impact on their electoral prospects. They may publicly express their views on the Federal Reserve's policies and advocate for certain measures that align with their political agenda. This can include calls for more accommodative monetary policy to stimulate economic growth or demands for tighter regulation to address perceived risks.

It is worth noting that while presidents and political candidates may voice their opinions on the Federal Reserve, they have limited direct control over its actions. The Federal Reserve operates independently from the executive branch, and its decisions are made by the Federal Open Market Committee (FOMC), which consists of appointed members. However, the president does have the power to nominate and appoint members to the Federal Reserve Board of Governors, which can indirectly shape the direction of the institution.

Over the years, there have been instances of presidential opposition to the Federal Reserve and its policies. One notable example is President John F. Kennedy, who reportedly had concerns about the Federal Reserve's influence on the economy and sought to curtail its power. However, his efforts to reform the Federal Reserve were cut short by his assassination in 1963, leaving the impact of his opposition unresolved.

Other presidents, such as Richard Nixon and Jimmy Carter, also expressed dissatisfaction with the Federal Reserve's policies during their respective administrations. Nixon famously criticized the Federal Reserve for its tight monetary policy, which he believed was hindering economic growth. Carter, on the other hand, faced the challenge of high inflation during his presidency and clashed with the Federal Reserve over its approach to combating inflation.

The outcomes of presidential opposition to the Federal Reserve have varied. While some presidents have been able to influence the direction of the institution through their appointments to the Board of Governors, others have faced resistance or limited success in their attempts to challenge the Federal Reserve's policies. Ultimately, the Federal Reserve's independence and its mandate to maintain price stability and promote maximum employment make it a complex institution to reform or control.

In conclusion, the Federal Reserve's impact on elections is primarily through its influence on the economy and public perception of economic conditions. Its control over monetary policy allows it to shape the economic landscape during election cycles, potentially benefiting or challenging the incumbent party. While presidents and political candidates may express their views on the Federal Reserve, their direct control over its actions is limited. The outcomes of presidential opposition to the Federal Reserve have varied, with some presidents able to shape the institution through appointments, while others have faced resistance. Understanding the Federal Reserve's impact on elections is crucial for comprehending the broader political dynamics surrounding monetary policy and financial regulation.

Conclusion

12.1 The Legacy of the Federal Reserve

The establishment of the Federal Reserve has had a profound impact on the United States and its economy. As we delve into the legacy of the Federal Reserve, it is crucial to understand the power dynamics that existed before its creation and how they shifted afterward. Additionally, we will explore the presidential opposition to the Federal Reserve and the outcomes of those challenges.

Power Dynamics Before the Federal Reserve

Before the creation of the Federal Reserve, the American people held a certain level of power over the government. One significant power they possessed was the ability to influence legislation through their elected representatives. The democratic system allowed citizens to voice their concerns and hold their representatives accountable for their actions.

Another crucial power the American people had was the ability to exercise veto power indirectly. By electing officials who aligned with their interests, the people could effectively veto policies they disagreed with. This power was derived from the democratic principles upon which the United States was founded.

The Loss of Power After the Federal Reserve

The establishment of the Federal Reserve brought about a significant shift in power dynamics. With the creation of a central bank, the control over monetary policy and the regulation of the banking system shifted away from the American people and into the hands of a select group of individuals. This shift resulted in a loss of direct influence over economic decisions.

The Federal Reserve, being an independent entity, operates with a certain level of autonomy. While it is subject to oversight by Congress, its decision-making process is not directly influenced by the American people. This lack of direct control over monetary policy has led to concerns about the concentration of power and the potential for decisions that may not align with the best interests of the general public.

Presidential Opposition to the Federal Reserve

John F. Kennedy (JFK) is often cited as a president who expressed opposition to the Federal Reserve. JFK's administration was marked by a desire to reduce the influence of the Federal Reserve and regain control over monetary policy. However, his efforts to challenge the Federal Reserve were cut short by his assassination in 1963, leaving the true extent of his opposition unclear.

Other presidents have also expressed concerns about the Federal Reserve and its impact on the economy. Presidents such as Woodrow Wilson, Franklin D. Roosevelt, and Richard Nixon have all made statements critical of the Federal Reserve's policies. However, despite their reservations, none of these presidents were able to successfully dismantle or significantly alter the Federal Reserve's structure.

Outcomes of Presidential Opposition

The opposition of presidents to the Federal Reserve has had limited success in bringing about substantial changes to the institution. While some presidents have voiced their concerns and attempted to exert influence over the Federal Reserve's policies, the central bank has largely maintained its independence and authority.

One outcome of presidential opposition has been increased scrutiny and public awareness of the Federal Reserve. The debates and discussions surrounding the institution have led to a greater understanding of its role and impact on the economy. However, in terms of structural changes or significant alterations to the Federal Reserve's operations, presidential opposition has not yielded substantial results.

It is important to note that the Federal Reserve's independence from direct political influence is intended to insulate it from short-term political pressures. This independence allows the Federal Reserve to make decisions based on long-term economic considerations rather than short-term political gains. However, it also raises questions about accountability and transparency, which we will explore further in subsequent sections.

In conclusion, the legacy of the Federal Reserve is one of a significant shift in power dynamics and the consolidation of authority over monetary policy and the banking system. The American people, who once held veto power indirectly through their elected representatives, have seen a reduction in their direct influence over economic decisions. While presidential opposition to the Federal Reserve has raised awareness and sparked debates, it has not resulted in substantial changes to the institution. The Federal Reserve's independence and authority remain intact, leaving questions about accountability and transparency for further examination.

12.2 The Importance of Understanding

Understanding the Federal Reserve and its impact on the American people is crucial in order to grasp the complexities of the modern financial system. The Federal Reserve, as we have explored throughout this book, plays a significant role in shaping the economy, influencing monetary policy, and regulating the banking system. However, the true history and implications of the Federal Reserve are often shrouded in mystery and misunderstood by the general public. In this section, we will emphasize the importance of understanding the Federal Reserve and its implications for the American people.

One of the key aspects of understanding the Federal Reserve is recognizing the power dynamics that existed before and after its creation. Prior to the establishment of the Federal Reserve, the American people had a certain level of power over the government, including the ability to exercise veto power. This power allowed the people to have a say in the decision-making process and act as a check on the government's actions. However, with the creation of the Federal Reserve, a significant portion of this power was transferred to a centralized authority.

The Federal Reserve Act of 1913 granted the Federal Reserve the authority to control the nation's monetary policy, including the regulation of interest rates and the money supply. This shift in power meant that decisions regarding the economy and financial system were no longer solely in the hands of the American people but were instead concentrated in the hands of a select few individuals within the Federal Reserve.

Despite the concentration of power within the Federal Reserve, there have been instances of presidential opposition to its existence and influence. One notable example is President John F. Kennedy, who sought to end the Federal Reserve and return the power to the American people. However, his efforts were ultimately unsuccessful, as he was assassinated before he could fully implement his plans. Other presidents, such as Andrew Jackson and Woodrow

Wilson, also expressed concerns about the Federal Reserve and its impact on the economy. However, their opposition did not result in the dissolution or significant reform of the Federal Reserve.

The outcome of presidential opposition to the Federal Reserve has varied throughout history. While some presidents have been vocal about their concerns, the Federal Reserve has remained largely intact and continues to exert its influence over the economy. This highlights the challenges faced by those who seek to challenge the Federal Reserve's power and the difficulty of implementing significant reforms.

Understanding the Federal Reserve and its implications is not only important for historical purposes but also for the present and future. The decisions made by the Federal Reserve have a direct impact on the economy, including factors such as inflation, interest rates, and economic crises. Without a comprehensive understanding of the Federal Reserve and its operations, it becomes difficult for the American people to fully comprehend the reasons behind economic fluctuations and the policies implemented to address them.

Moreover, understanding the Federal Reserve is crucial for individuals to make informed decisions about their personal finances. The Federal Reserve's control over interest rates, for example, directly affects borrowing costs, mortgage rates, and the overall cost of living. By understanding the Federal Reserve's role in the economy, individuals can better navigate financial decisions and plan for their future.

Furthermore, understanding the Federal Reserve is essential for holding it accountable. The lack of transparency surrounding the Federal Reserve has been a subject of criticism and concern. Without a clear understanding of its operations, it becomes challenging for the American people to assess the Federal Reserve's actions and ensure that it is acting in the best interest of the public. By demanding transparency and accountability, the American people can play a more active role in shaping the policies and decisions of the Federal Reserve.

In conclusion, the importance of understanding the Federal Reserve cannot be overstated. It is crucial for individuals to comprehend the history, power dynamics, and implications of the Federal Reserve in order to make informed decisions, hold it accountable, and actively participate in shaping the future of the American economy. By gaining a deeper understanding of the Federal Reserve, the American people can empower themselves and contribute to a more transparent and equitable financial system.

12.3 Moving Forward

As we conclude our exploration of the Federal Reserve and its impact on the American economy and society, it is crucial to consider the path forward. The Federal Reserve has been a subject of intense debate and scrutiny since its inception, with proponents arguing for its necessity in maintaining economic stability and opponents questioning its power and influence. Moving forward, it is essential to reflect on the lessons learned and consider potential reforms or alternatives to ensure a more transparent and accountable financial system.

One of the key aspects to address when moving forward is understanding the power dynamics that existed before and after the establishment of the Federal Reserve. Prior to its creation, the American people had a more direct influence on the government through mechanisms such as veto power. The checks and balances provided by the Constitution allowed for a more decentralized decision-making process, with power distributed among the executive, legislative, and judicial branches. However, with the establishment of the Federal Reserve, a significant portion of monetary policy and financial regulation was consolidated into the hands of a few appointed officials. This centralization of power led to a loss of direct influence for the American people over economic matters.

While President John F. Kennedy is often associated with opposition to the Federal Reserve, he was not the only president to express concerns about its influence. Other presidents, such as Andrew Jackson and Woodrow Wilson, also questioned the role and power of central banks. However, their efforts to challenge or dismantle the Federal Reserve were met with limited success. The outcome of presidential opposition to the Federal Reserve has been largely ineffective in bringing about significant structural changes. The Federal Reserve has remained a powerful institution, largely insulated from political interference.

Moving forward, it is crucial to consider the potential reforms or alternatives to the current system. One proposal that has gained traction is the call for increased transparency and accountability within the Federal Reserve. Critics argue that the lack of transparency surrounding the decision-making processes and operations of the Federal Reserve undermines public trust and confidence. Advocates for reform suggest implementing measures such as regular audits of the Federal Reserve to ensure greater accountability to the American people.

Another area of focus for moving forward is the relationship between the Federal Reserve and the banking system. The Federal Reserve plays a crucial role in regulating and supervising banks, but concerns have been raised about the extent of its control over the banking system. Some argue for a reevaluation of the current banking regulations and the role of the Federal Reserve in order to strike a better balance between stability and innovation within the financial sector.

Additionally, the Federal Reserve's role in the global economy should be carefully examined. As the United States' central bank, its actions and policies have far-reaching implications beyond national borders. Moving forward, it is important to consider the impact of Federal Reserve decisions on global markets and collaborate with international partners to ensure stability and fairness in the global financial system.

Furthermore, the critiques and controversies surrounding the Federal Reserve should not be dismissed but rather addressed in a constructive manner. It is essential to engage in open and informed discussions about the Federal Reserve's role, its decision-making processes, and the potential consequences of its policies. By fostering a more inclusive and transparent dialogue, we can work towards a better understanding of the Federal Reserve's operations and its impact on the economy and society.

Ultimately, moving forward requires active participation and engagement from the American people. Public perception and awareness of the Federal Reserve should be encouraged and enhanced through educational initiatives and accessible information. By empowering individuals with knowledge and understanding, we can foster a more informed citizenry that can actively participate in shaping the future of the Federal Reserve and the financial system as a whole.

In conclusion, the Federal Reserve remains a complex and influential institution in the United States. Moving forward, it is crucial to reflect on the lessons learned from its history and consider potential reforms or alternatives to ensure a more transparent, accountable, and inclusive financial system. By engaging in open dialogue, promoting transparency, and empowering the American people, we can work towards a future where the Federal Reserve serves the best interests of the nation and its citizens.